The Music Machine

The Music Machine

BY ROGER KARSHNER

Nash Publishing, Los Angeles

Library of Congress Catalog Card Number: 79-167529
Standard Book Number: 8402-1242-9

Published simultaneously in the United States and Canada
by Nash Publishing Corporation, 9255 Sunset Boulevard,
Los Angeles, California 90069.

Printed in the United States of America

First printing

DEDICATED TO

*all of the good people in the record
industry—the fine, honest people
who are the cement that holds the whole
scary mess together.*

Contents

The Music Machine

1
Dynamic
Enthusiastic
Excitement

Dynamic, that's what the record business is. It's enthusiasm and excitement, too, dynamic, enthusiastic excitement at all levels. The hype is the thing—the motivator; the ever-present element that kicks the ass of the industry. Everybody enthused—dynamic—excited about everything. . . . Luncheons are dynamic and charged with excitement. Business dinners are pungent with excitement, and smiling, positive people grin over steak to win negative games. Every nook and cranny of the industry is stuffed with little people who spend their best energies on being energized. All situations are treated with the same level of positiveness because, after all, "Ain't that the stuff that made America great?"

Coffee breaks are dynamic, too, with a lump of enthusiasm and a dash of excitement. During rest room visits, kidneys are relieved with grunts of positive joy, and even the urinals seem to bubble with excitement. Managers and artists, publishers and agents, attorneys and promotion men, sales reps and sales managers, producers and executives, and stock boys, shipping clerks and presidents, are all positive—dynamic.

Sales meetings are conducted with dynamic thrust by dynamic people. Entire rooms of superenthused reps sit excited over table tops covered with green felt cloth. Before them are pitchers of dynamic ice water and regimented placements of 3 x 5 note pads and No. 2 Ticonderoga pencils. Blackboards abound with dynamic figures that spell "dollars" and "objectives" and "quotas." Cigarette smoke, exhaled with puffs of enthusiasm, hangs over the proceedings like silver-grey gossamer, causing attendees to choke on their own excitement. Pointers are pointed by sales managers with pointed heads. Plans are laid with the stealth and commitment of maurauding pirates, all gathered 'round a cryptic master plan, with ball point pens clenched in their teeth. Slide shows split the dark with flashlight fingers of dynamism, while hangover eyes photograph each frame with blinks of excitement. Speeches are made and points are driven home by fist-pounding fanatics. Success stories are told about sales conquests by steely-eyed, hard-hitting, aggresive young zealots. Applause rises and rises as each story is spilled because everyone applauds at and for everthing in the spirit of dynamic sales-repism.

Sales cocktail parties buzz with excitement over new product—all new product. Glasses clink and salesmen drink and dynamic toasts are proposed to such "meaningful" endeavors as "hitting quotas at all cost" and "snowing that little dealer in Altoona." Nothing is ever questioned because everything is so exciting. Wrongs are buried because, after all, wrongs are negative and positive people don't recognize negatives.

Artists, too, are positive. They're positive because they're "talented" people with dynamic personalities. Everything in their world is exciting. They're excited about openings. They're excited about tours. They're excited about their latest recording. They're excited about new houses; new toupees and new wives. They're excited about television appearances. They're excited about movie potentials. They're excited about politics and Vietnam and sports and "the youth." They're excited about sales, cover art, astrology and bowel regularity. Effervescent, enthusiastic artists take dynamic pills and the excitement continues.

Promotion men make dynamic pitches to enthusiastic programmers. Every recording is "exciting" and is presented with finger popping enthusiasm. Every item is a hit. Every artist's record is better than the one before. Everyone's excited. Promotional orgies are dynamic and the hookers are enthusiastic because the clients are excited. Wonderful wine and wonderful wisecracks create exciting relationships that help the promoters "get next to" the broadcast dynamos. Promotion men's mouths run four-minute miles, rattling positive gossip about negative people. Enthusiastic reports are communicated with positive excitement to dynamic, national offices. All the news is positive—ever positive because nothing is ever negative in a world where wrongs are always right. The potential for air play is always positive and all departments work on the positive futures, projecting fearlessly with excitable conviction.

Salesmen sell with positive purpose. They run excitedly into buyers' offices and shake hands with dynamic sincerity.

Order blanks are whipped out with flourish and resolution in a gesture that "means business." All dynamic sales people "mean business," and business' best friend is the dynamic salesman—the man in the field—the Horatio Alger of hits. Quotas are "busted" by excitement. Sales are closed by excitement. Business is built by excitement. Excitement is contagious and a dynamic salesman is the man who spreads the germ.

Producers are very excited. Even when they're depressed, they're excited. Yes, they're excited over their depression because it represents a most dynamic period from which existing work has erupted. Their lives are a succession of dynamic depressions. Every new production is the most exciting production ever produced by any producer. Enthusiastic people are forced to listen to new "dynamic" productions. They react with enthusiasm and dance and gyrate, and pull their sideburns. Everyone's always excited about all new productions and the producers grow even more dynamic in the wonderful world of music where all productions are great.

Art directors are always enthused by new exciting product. They create exciting covers to package the musical masterpieces. Reds and blues are enthusiastically blended into exciting shades of green. Abstractions tumble from ink wells and paste jars. Cameras click grainy nudes; acrylics flow into psychedelic sex and collages are overlaid faster than the models. Exciting, dramatic trick bags are geared to the "hip" consumer tastes. New shapes and exciting designs, dramatically increase consumer prices. The music doesn't change, but the price does. But, the covers are exciting and dynamic, in keeping with the industry enthusiasm.

Merchandising aids are really exciting. All those divider cards and wall streamers, mobiles, dummy album covers and the special newspaper ad mats are truly dynamic. Each little record shop gimmick is truly a masterpiece. Everyone oohs and aahs with enthusiasm at every cardboard cutout and pop-up display. Real excitement. Sales is excited. Promotion, artists and managers are thrilled. Yes, creativity runs wild because the merchandising people are excited, so very excited and so very enthused—regular Picassos, sitting around on their dynamic butts dreaming up unusable pieces of excitement.

Publishers puff fantastic, dynamic cigars as they propel promotions via exciting phone calls. Restless men, devoted to all that is right and proper, working for the betterment of industrykind. Short, heavyset, bald eagles, with gold dust in their hearts, talk enthusiastically about all their exciting material. Never a bad lyric; never a weak melody; just masterworks. Oh, what excitement . . . such excitement!

And the dynamic excitement roars on. Promotion is excited by dynamic sales and sales is excited by the enthusiasm of merchandising excitement. Excitedly, producers project dynamic enthusiasm into their artists, who positively convey the positive dynamics injected by producers into the art directors, who are captured by the excitement that has excited the artists. Around, it goes—excitement, enthusiasm, dynamics, circling out of reach and control ahead of the collective body of industy idiots that ignited this pinwheel of stupidity.

These phony, positive interrelationships are industry chain letters no one dares to break. Those who try are branded as negative troublemakers, pessimists. So, enthusiastic lies are told. Dynamic mistakes are perpetuated and phony excitement abounds, and on and on it spins, a whirling mass of self-deception, rushing into infinity, pulling the industry helplessly in its wake.

2
Misfits and Me

"Hello, Mr. Karshner. You don't know me but my name is Bob Stone."

This innocent introduction that spilled from my telephone receiver one morning in October 1963 propelled me into one of my most insane record business involvements.

Bob Stone was a local musician, who had been beating around the rock-club circuit in the city for some time. He headed a group I shall call "The Misfits." Bob and his group were really musical down-and-outers who drifted from one sub-scale date to another. In the course of this drifting, the guys somehow, by the grace of God, uncovered sufficient money to underwrite a basic three-hour recording session. So armed with a legion of nondescript musical personnel, Bob Stone and The Misfits invaded the recording studios, and their song was recorded spontaneously under the three-hour AFM session deadline.

The morning following this now-famous happening, I received a call from leader, Bob Stone.

"Hello, Mr. Karshner. You don't know me but my name is Bob Stone."

Bob proceeded to unfold the story of his recording date, how he had been directed to call me by a mutual acquaintance, my attorney, Gino Capozzi, for advice and counsel relative to the handling and exploitation of his recorded master. I tried my best to discourage Bob. I told him how many times I had been approached in this regard and how in every case I was appalled by the crap that I had auditioned. I told him I did not have either the time or the inclination to review his material.

But Stone persisted. He implored me to give him just a few moments. I firmly rejected his insistence upon a personal meeting but did agree to extend him the courtesy of a telephone listen.

I braced myself for at least three minutes of musical chaos. After a brief period of adjusting levels for telephone, Stone started the record. I listened. Over the lines came a spirited and solid rock masterpiece. The sonofabitch had cut a hit.

I instructed Stone to leave a dub at my office so I could further analyze the work on professional playback equipment. That afternoon I relistened to the master on a good system. It was great! The sonofabitch had sure enough cut a hit.

That evening I contacted Gino. I gold him Bob had called at his instruction and that I had heard his master and I believed it was a hit record. I suggested that he and I form a partnership and undertake the master placement, as well as represent The Misfits as a management team. He agreed and within one week The Misfits were signed to Gino and me for exclusive artist management.

Shortly after the management agreement was negotiated, I rushed a dub of the master to the home office of the company for which I was working. I indicated to my company that I thought the master was great, and if they were interested they should contact Mr. Gino Capozzi.

And behind the scenes I was doing my number. I was stirring up windmills of hype within my company. Every time I telephoned the home office I laid on mountains of positive information about The Misfits, and the sensational master that had been submitted. The entire West Coast operation was turned on to The Misfits master. I indicated that other major record companies were scrambling to pick up the record, that Bob Stone was a genius, that the group was the most electrifying act ever to plug in amplifiers. The energy of my approach mounted with each call and The Misfits began to loom as recording giants in the minds of my company's A & R directors. After about two weeks of my verbal accolades, plus Gino's persistence, the company agreed to purchase the master for one thousand dollars. In a flury of ballpoint madness, contracts were signed. The Misfits were now a real live recording act, signed to a major recording company.

After the artists' contracts were signed, a massive structuring job began. I believed the record was great and I knew that if it did become a national hit the group would be demanded for live performances. Most young rock groups drown in the wake of record success because they are totally unprepared to perform live, and professional live performance is essential to artist development and longevity. It's also a very lucrative aspect. So I rented space in a cheap walkup to audition and rehearse my pygmalion.

The first audition was a nightmare—everyone out of tune, out of time and out to lunch. There was no show sense, timing or professionalism. The guys looked bad and sounded bad, but despite all the negatives there was a certain earthy magnetism about the group. So we started to rehearse.

First an act had to be written, so I scribbled together a show outline. The leader really lacked personality projection, so I decided to focus upon the lead singer, who was a trim, appealing, black-haired Macedonian kid. He was uniquely talented and had tremendous potential, but he had to be prodded and cajoled into working. He rejected all suggestions and had to be painstakingly sold on every point, and then resold. He never ever really accepted and absorbed instructions.

The other group members were also problem children. The trumpet player was laconic and lacked responsiveness. The guitar player, who was the best musician, really wasn't sure if he wanted to remain part of the group. He had been "picked up" for the recording session and retained as an unofficial member. The bass player was a Swede—a nice guy but was hung up on the term "definitely," which he injected at the oddest times. "How's your cold?" "Definitely."

Anyway, I had five unsophisticated guys with raw musical abilities to polish and groom.

I worked up an entire show. Special introduction, patter and choreography. Special effects were also introduced, and attention was given to material, tempo and timing. We worked out nearly every day in spite of the childish conflicts, tardiness and general internal chaos between the group members.

Meanwhile, my partner was involving himself with the administrative and organizational aspects. He was a good man, not the typical legal type. Wasn't pompous and was totally honest. I still trust him with my life. Gino was one of the good ones.

Things were developing reasonably well. The group was beginning to respond to the daily sessions, and some order was beginning to evolve. And all this on spec, mind you. All of this preparation, planning and effort was being expended before the record was released. Release date yet unknown. So at this time we were gambling time and money on the feeling for a record. What calculated insantiy!

My company finally informed Gino that the record would be released in mid-December. I panicked. Releasing a record near the Holidays can be disasterous. Christmas music programming and general promotional lethargy usually spell anonymity for a new product released at this time. Aware of the Holiday record mortality rate I asked for postponement of release. The group members rebelled. It hit the fan. They came at me from all sides, like sharks. How could I hold up the release? They had been waiting and rehearsing for two months. Their wives, girlfriends, neighbors, creditors (especially creditors) were waiting. I held my ground. I knew my decision was proper. They kept bitching, but I held fast.

Gino was busy smoothing over problems—money problems—and I kept the group rehearsing, kept shining up the act, kept shifting, sifting and changing. Our guitar player finally decided to resign. So we recruited a new group member as replacement. He was a fair lead instrumentalist, very quiet and shy. A reticent, little fellow, who's music paralleled his personality. We kept rehearsing.

The record was finally released on January 17, 1964. Hardly a red-letter day, but to us then it was Christmas, New Years and Thanksgiving combined. All of our rehearsals, time, money and effort were preparation for this. Nearly four months of labor pains for the birth of an innocuous piece of vinyl.

I rushed the record to the two local Top-40 radio stations. The programmers were close friends of mine. Good men, both now out of the business. Without hesitation the record went on the air and they played the hell out of it. At first no reaction, then on about the third day of air play the requests began to roll in. Soon the listener demand was in avalanche proportions. Record shops were also beginning to get consumer calls. It was starting to happen. Public reaction was the same as mine had been that dreary morning in October. That sonofabitch, Bob Stone, had sure enough cut a hit.

Requests kept pouring in and record shops were being deluged with calls for the record. The manufacturer started pumping stock into the market to meet the demand. I kept selling and promoting and rehearsing the fingers off of The Misfits.

Within two weeks I was successful in getting air play on another key radio station in an adjacent major market. The hit pattern unfolded there, also. Great listener response, solid consumer requests and sales. I knew we had a hit record. Now there was no doubt, so I kept promoting. I picked up air play on all the radio outlets in my territory. I forced sales and personally merchandised the record at consumer level, and I kept rehearsing The Misfits.

Gino, meanwhile, buoyed by our success, made more personal financial investments. He advanced money for first-rate instruments, amplifiers, speakers, microphones and public address systems. He even purchased a Chevy van to transport equipment and The Misfits to their play dates. He was supplying the funds out of pocket, gambling on the regional reaction, and I was supplying the energy to obtain more air play and sales.

The record exploded in both of my major markets. It reached the number-one position in both cities and held the top spot, unchallenged, for five consecutive weeks. Sales in my region exceeded sixty thousand units. An absolute regional blockbuster.

At this point my company still had no knowledge of my association with The Misfits. They were thrilled by the regional results and complimentary that I'd "steered them on to a good record," but as far as they were concerned Gino was the sole management. They were excited, happy and flattering, but weren't convinced, however, The Misfit's record had national potential. It was just, they thought, a good "regional hit." Typical industry shortsightedness.

Neither my philosophy nor my hidden interest would allow me to accept this negative, narrow view. Regional hit, indeed. That thinking is invalid. It was then, and still is. Markets tend to be homogenous and public taste in similar markets generally agree. "Regional hit" thinking is an industry cliché, arising out of the industry's inability to successfully spread records over wide areas simultaneously.

Goaded by my ego I began my own national promotional campaign. Armed with my regional success story I set out to conquer the nation. I literally lived on the telephone. I called every disc jockey, program director and music director in the United States. I solicited help from my fellow promoters. I bugged the trades, lists, dealers, one-stops and rack jobbers. My phone bill for three weeks was $1,000. And I kept going. I directed stock into markets. I personally took orders from local record outlets all across the country. I even solved a few bad credit problems to wheedle in quantities of our record.

Night after night, day after day, I lived by the telephone. Hotels, bars, restaurants, clubs, neighbor's patios, dentist's offices, stock rooms, radio stations became my offices. I took and placed calls any time, any place, anywhere. The pace was quick-silver. I lost thirteen pounds in thirty days and developed a twitch in the left side of my neck.

Our first big break came when a station in Baltimore added the record to their play list. This action established the record outside the psychological "regional" barrier. Next, Philadelphia: and The Misfits were on their way. The record entered the national trade chart race at the very bottom, 100, and then it began to climb. My efforts and Gino's gambling were beginning to pay off.

Requests for The Misfits began to pour in. Suddenly the guys with no talent, who played humiliating jobs for below union scale, were in demand. "Overnight," Bob Stone was a genius. Every little chick in the country wanted to lay the lead singer. Our Swedish bassist became a sex symbol. Suddenly the world began to bloom around The Misfits. Bookings were mounting and so was our price, and we signed the boys with a major booking agent to professionally negotiate the booking details.

The hours of rehearsing and preparation paid off big. For once, a rock group was prepared to resurrect live the recorded performance. We had polished the act to a high gloss. Bows, intros, bridges and patter were delivered with succinct continuity. They were ready. The Misfits first major appearance was in Milwaukee. They shared the bill with "name" acts. They stole the show.

National air play was expanding. Sales were multiplying and chart listings growing. So were our problems with The

Misfits. Problems, those inevitable problems that permeate rock musicianship were beginning to fester.

As the record climbed the national charts, bookings rolled in. Offers of twelve hundred, fifteen hundred, and two thousand dollars per concert. We booked The Misfits, through our agent, into the best rock clubs. They were traveling and working four and five dates per week. Their performances were professional and bred new bookings. At one point we booked the group as part of a national tour where they would get wide exposure. They were enthusiastically received by large audiences in major metropolitan areas around the nation. Popularity was swelling and records were selling.

My company was ecstatic over the success of The Misfits. Wild-eyed with profit visions over a group they had, two months earlier, relegated to the level of "regional hit status." Now, however, the P & L minds of the 50 percent gross-margin boys were being illuminated by the reflection of a new comet in their artist's skies. Much attention was being given to the "group's welfare."

My management association with the group unfolded with gathering rapidity. My activity and involvement was too demanding not to become apparent, so I made a full disclosure to my company regarding my 50 percent management affiliation. They feigned surprise and pleasure and immediately began relating to me on a very special level. After all, I was now one of the big cannons behind successful recording artists. All the executives became Mr. Condescending and communicated with real big business, slap-back cordiality. I was a "heavyweight." Why, they knew it all along. Strange world. Just five months before I had been considered a rebellious record freak.

On two occasions executives flew in to "see me," to see if
"everything was ok?" I was offered a standard tie-up production deal, which I rejected. "No, Massa," I said, kicking a
horse turd. "I'z gwanna stay rat 'cheer and do ma' lil' ole'
prooomotion job and manage ma' lil' ole' reecordin' group.
An dats dee truff."

Bob Stone was unhappy with the trumpet player, so Gino
fired him. He had been a pick-up musician and was not part
of The Misfits group contract. Of course he sued us. Everybody sues everybody else in the rock group-management
fellowship. It's standard practice. Law suits and counter suits
are dealt out with gin rummy casualness, because everyone's
screwed up and scared and insecure. He was replaced by a
little Armenian kid who hopped around all over the stage like
a chimp.

With the record now fast approaching the top 30 on all the
national charts, it was time to record a "pickup" album and a
new single. Pickup albums are recorded in the wake of a hit
single record. So recording budgets were approved and we
began planning the album. Material, original and other, had
to be written and selected and rehearsals had to be held
preliminary to actual recordings. Getting The Misfits to plan
or organize anything was next to impossible. Rehearsals were
jokes. A lot of nonsense, pizza, beer and farting around.
Endless, tedious, unproductive hours were wasted. Rehearsals
were busts.

Once in the recording studio, things degenerated to even a
lower level of disorganization. Hour after hour of costly
studio time was pissed away while the group pieced together
each musical selection—a note here, a chord, peep and honk
there. Days were spent in the studios. Lunches and dinners
were brought in and we ate like prisoners while the musical

marathon dragged on. And then there were bickerings, tantrums and disagreements.

After a long vigil, I finally squeezed the album out of The Misfits. This album contained the second single record which was a follow-up success to their initial hit. By the way: The Misfits first and most successful record climbed to Number Five on the national charts and sold in excess of 725,000 copies.

By this time, I was deeply embroiled in the group's managerial affairs. The day-to-day problems demanded instant attention and more and more of my energy was being diverted to that end. Gino, likewise, was being forced to neglect his law practice. Publishing considerations had to be deliberated. Bookings had to be negotiated. Sales and promotion support and monitoring was necessary. A fan club had to be organized. Press and publicity lines had to be inflated. The Misfits were becoming big business.

Gino was Mr. Inside, I, Mr. Outside. He handled the legal, financial and bookkeeping matters and I functioned as promotion man, producer-coordinator, press agent and father confessor to the group's ailments, which were many.

Singles and albums were selling well and bookings were more frequent and lucrative. The Misfits were becoming an important industry name. My company was now investing heavily in the group's future and the substantial marketing program was cementing the group's image at the consumer level. Money was beginning to pour in and in spite of the group's inconsistencies, I could smell a golden-lined future. The time had come for a personal decision. In the summer of 1964 I resigned my regional post to devote my total energies to the management of The Misfits.

Ensconced in my managerial role, I was free to detonate a

promotion attack that would blow the group into the eternal "big time." What I didn't realize then was that there is no eternal big time on the rocky roads of rock. There's only fleeting big time, flash-in-the-pan fame and eternal bullshit. But, anyway, I started my juices in motion. I dug into the management manure with gusto. Promotions, merchandising, sales, air play, bookings, press, fan club. I assaulted them all. I cut a swath of super-energized hype and hoopla. It paid off, too. People listened because I represented a hit recording group. Magic words, "hit recording group."

Record Number Three was another hit. Boy, were we sailing. Business was marvelous and I was elated. Golden Boy had done it again. I was so thrilled, I bought a new Porsche. I also bought some new clothes—very mod and very hip to encase the brainy body of such a magnificent management potentate. My star was on the rise and the sun was shining down like a big blue dot flashbulb taking 8 x 10 glossies of a wonderful world. What I failed to notice, though, were the long, long shadows that were being cast. Yes, fall was in the air for Gino, Roger and The Misfits.

For some time, problems had been chewing away at the group's unity, slowly and insidiously causing irreparable damage. Old conflicts remained unresolved, and, as time wore on, they became bitternesses that created permanent divisevness.

Inevitably, there evolved a group-management deadlock. The Misfits refused to accept bookings. They rejected recording supervision. They felt our management controls were too stringent and percentages excessive. In short, "they didn't need us anymore." Another rock legend bit the dust, and The Misfits went to that big record hop in the sky.

3
Record Promotion for Fun and Nausea

In cities . . . live titans. These titans are programming gods. They are the essence of format broadcasting. They are absolute—supreme. Like mighty thundering overlords, they rule radio empires. They mold trends and knead the public's musical tastes into balls of rotten snot.

Sounds like storybook fiction, doesn't it? Well, I'm sorry, bit it ain't. There are such men and they do have control over national radio networks that have meaningful impact upon the musical tastes of the country. The power these men wield and the way record industry people relate to them make fascinating and frightening stories. We'll call these programmers, "Big Broadcasters." Now, Big Broadcasters are responsible for programming more than one radio station. Big Broadcasters have total authority; and even though the stations maintain their own program managers and music directors, Big Broadcasters still have the final word in the areas of music, jingles and all aspects that pertain to the station's on-the-air "sound."

Big Broadcasters oversee all of their stations with cautious scrutiny. Every programming aspect is analyzed to assure adherence to the tenants they lay down as programming gospel. Their word is law and they enforce their dictates with relish and determination. All stations are monitored as police actions against individuality. A certain "sound standard" is demanded (sort of like quality control without quality.) All jockeys must sound similar. An on-air tightness is a requisite.

Big Broadcasters also make recommendations regarding disc jockey hirings and firings. They have powerful influence over the stations they program. After all, their job is to unravel broadcasting tangles and to establish their outlets as rating winners. And they show gains. Their methods get results. These shouting, screaming, promoting electronic P.T. Barnums always stir up ratings by pandering at the lowest levels.

Of course, every piece of recorded material that is played by their affiliates must be sanctioned by the programming octopi. Nothing goes on the air unless it passes their demographic (people statistics) tests. To program the wrong record and get listener tune-out is a cardinal sin. The records must be right. They must be proven to be demographically sound.

You know, formaters program to demographics. They don't give a damn about the record, the music. All they care about is that the selection is demographically suited for particular listener segments of their broadcast day. If the ambiguous, demographic measurements indicate that more housewives are listening to the station at a particular time, the programmer concentrates "housewife" music into that segment. If the measurement indicates a time heavily weighted to teens, more "teen" music is played during that period. Now, how the hell these novocain brains can separate music like nuts and bolts, I'll never understand. What the hell's a housewife record? What in heaven's name is teenage music?

But anyway, Big Broadcasters control what records go into the broadcast hopper at their stations. They're musical Zeuses, these guys—ones who can virtually make or break talent. Millions of dollars, futures of corporations, jobs, hopes, dreams rise and fall on their musical decisions, and they are feared by the industry.

Promotional people bootlick these guys with the timidity of stray dogs. They exist in eternal fear they will offend them and fall into disfavor. Anybody who can get next to these nabobs will assure his own industry success. Promotion men who are favorably associated receive raises, promotions and kid-glove handling. No superior would dare mistreat a subordinate who is "close to" a broadcast giant, regardless of provocation. The fellow could be a thief, an ax murderer, and receive full pardon. Conversely, not being "close to" a biggee is precarious, and being an adversary—no matter how justifiably—will result in immediate dismissal. I've seen it happen. Excellent men, hardworking, intelligent, thoroughly loyal and honest people have been summarily terminated or demoted due to an unfavorable episode. Not being next to or "close" is regarded as weakness and failure, all reasons aside.

"Getting next to" is difficult because Big Broadcasters must filter every association with the precision of chemists, for any hint of dishonesty or leak of inconsistency would mean their ruin.

Many Big Broadcasters are honest people. But there are bad apples that taint the programming barrel. Yes, there are

Big Broadcasters who have built-in systems which allow corruption to seep in while leaving an illusion of purity. They subtly and indirectly intimidate the manufacturers for payola kick-backs. Their means are crafty and quiet. They leave no scent. And these stealthy programming foxes raid the manufacturers' hen houses while the industry watchdogs sit helplessly by cowering, with their self-respect between their legs.

So kiddies, that's the way it is. Big Broadcasters are big cogs in the music machine. Cogs that get gobs of industry grease.

Restrictiveness of Top-40 air play in relation to the flood of record releases creates a very pressurized condition, and breaking through the hide of the Top-40 animal is a difficult task—one that necessitates dishonesty combined with the procedural pragmatism of market manipulation. Let me briefly outline here the air-play-to-release realities that currently exist as a grim industry specter. At this writing my facts are accurate.

There are 181 key Top-40 radio stations in the United States. This total breaks into two distinct related factors: primary and secondary.

There are 51 primary stations. These stations are located in 24 major market cities. These 24 areas represent 54 percent of the effective buying income of the nation compared to the next 300 towns, hamlets and villages combined. In these cities are located the "primary radio giants"; stations that effect instant mass local and national record sales. These Top-40 prime outlets demand the utmost promotional attention.

So, primarily, industry promotion is concerned with 51 stations in 24 markets.

Next, there are the 130 secondary and subsecondary markets that represent substantial buying income and/or are potential record development stations. "Starting" records via the secondary route is "back door promotion" but can be a methodically effective means of catalyzing single record sales.

So, in reality, there are currently 181 key radio stations in America that significantly contribute to the success of single record air play and sales. That's it. Fifty-one primary and 130 other.

Now, approximately 130 new singles are poured out weekly by all labels, and Top-40 stations only program about 35 records, 95 percent of which are established artist identities. You can see the near impossibility of breaking new material by new artists. A problem situation for an industry still relating to yesterday, employing yesterday's manpower, yesterday's methods and living by yesterday's clichés.

Now, the job of promotion is to massage this network of key radio outlets. In every major market, manufacturers employ their own promotion men and/or independent promotional people to bug the primary and secondary Top-40 stations. These guys spend their adult lives attempting to "get next to the key jocks," "get picks" and "break records." They utilize payola, layola, freebies, trade picks, regional picks, charts, advertising pressures and market information to hypo air play. They're salesmen, pimps, entertainers, buyers and criers. They have supple faces and can feign many moods—minstrels cavorting and cajoling for fun and profit.

At the national level lie the nerve centers of the promotional market game. National offices operate on a level with "boiler rooms," and information is gathered and dissiminated with carnival theatrics. The national promotional offices maintain large check sheets containing the call letters and market locations of the key 181 radio stations. Each record selection which is being "worked" is assigned one of these station check sheets. When a selection is added to any of the key station play lists, a checkmark is made adjacent to the station call letters. Subsequent entries are made to perpetuate a current status record throughout its air play life.

All records released are not given the same promotional attention—in fact, most records receive only courtesy promotional mailings. Separate, phony cover-up status information is maintained, however, to placate artists, producers, publishers and managers. Promotional personnel, however, always indicate "equal industry" on all products released. Artists and managers are the constant victims of the big promotional lie as the promotors at all levels create damaging illusion by their crooked enthusiasm.

As the air play information comes in from the field, the national office makes its marks and feeds back the latest information regarding the status of play. Market is pitted against market in order to fill the squares. Promotion men use the record's success story to impress and motivate any of their stations who are reluctant to program a selection. It's actually musical bingo—the object being to fill in enough squares to get a meaningful representation of key air play that will create station interaction. It's called "record spreading."

Obviously, the 51 major market giants are the springboards to instant hitdom. Any combination of these biggees will do it. Air play in New York, Detroit, Philadelphia, for example, will usually assure a record's success. But, the big ones are tough so the industry romances the secondaries. The idea here is to capture a multitude of secondary market play which will impress and "force" the megalopolis giants to program the selection. So, the companies go after the smaller stations in order to spark the monsters. And the monsters couldn't care less about the industry or the small broadcasters. They just sit back and burp. Record companies go after the key stations with laughable business seriousness. "All stops are pulled," to quote an industry platitude. Big dollars are dropped for lies.

A lot of industry dough is wasted on programming services publications. These publications are referred to as "sheets" or "lists." These sheets are broadcast spin-offs created to assist programmers in selecting demographically sound recorded material. New music is reviewed and critiqued and national information regarding audience response, sales reactions and record potentials and longevities is culled and refined into tip sheet form. These lists are sold by subscription to programmers and record manufacturers. The sheets are published weekly.

In view of the restrictiveness of Top-40 radio, these sheets have become an important industry tool. Favorable "picks" and mentions are golden because they alert programmers to the hit-potential of new products. So, the manufacturers engage in all sorts of chicanery to get good press.

Generally, each of the 181 key Top-40 stations subscribe to broadcast chart sheets. As subscribers, they also contribute weekly feedback relative to new record additions, requests and sales. Now, due to industry's subscriptions, the manufacturer's promotional organizations know exactly which stations report and who the correspondents are. They go after these correspondents with the grace of charging rhinos. Every conceivable method—lie—ploy—ruse—is brought into play. Markets are loaded with product and accounts bribed to report socko consumer reaction to the station which will, hopefully, communicate these "successes" to the sheets, which will publish information having favorable impact upon the other broadcast subscribers.

Promotional machines descend like swooping buzzards upon the more vulnerable secondary market radio stations for listings. Secondary, and particularly, demi-market stations, are used heartlessly for their "sheet" and "list" connections. Companies don't really give one damn for the small broadcasters. Oh sure, they talk openly about the importance of small stations and how the secondaries are the salvation of an industry crippled by the major market giants, but it's all hippy-dippy bull. They're just ear kissing the little guys, using them, patting ass, to generate chart-sheet feedback and capture the brass ring of major market air play. Because the major markets sell the records in the quantities that make million sellers, they have the buying power. All that the tiny market stations have are "list" affiliations; and the sharptoothed promotional hypocrites rip away at their carcasses for bits of listings.

Lists and sheets pop up all over the face of the industry because the industry supports such nonsense. It's always fearful of offending some jerk who may be "next to" someone who'll someday become a biggee with a "big sheet." So, everyone gets into the list act. Disc jockeys, promotion men, and tradesters start lists and get rich.

Some guys are nothing more than gossip peddlers. They are the industry's garbage disposal. They evolve into industry powers. Manufacturers pay them as much as five hundred dollars per week just to "be on their side." They falsify information, create phony enthusiasm for mediocre product and stir up, pass and perpetuate gossip. They blow like a big wind down the canyons of deceit.

List publishers also become all-knowing antiseptic ana-
lyzers of the product they review. They applaud and condemn with the authority of self-appointed visionaries.
Political issues become a regular feature of their outpouring,
and they editorialize with the fervor of Tom Paine, and lapse
into a da da created by their own misunderstanding and
ineptness. They pick little-known records in attempts to
prove their left-field "hit spotting" abilities. Trends are ex-
amined and projected. Casual references to industry executive personnel are frequent as special interviews with the
company heads are conducted and "probing questions" are
asked to "imperative problems." When industry people visit
list publishers at their headquarters, it's done with great
reverence as if they've at last found the meaning of life after
long celibacy and search. They pay homage to these phony
industry institutions with all of their typical dirt-kicking
obsequiousness.

List manipulation is a daily promotional custom and
strengthens all the other hypo practices which generate hits
and trends. All the various means of generating air play are
used from time to time. They're necessary to "get something
started." So, like priming a pump, these little inducements
are applied to start the flow. One such inducement is a
primer called "exclusives."

Exclusives are "hot" artist's recordings that are given to
only one radio station in a market. This is done frequently
for several reasons. As barter and trade for air play on
another recording; or as a favor to "get next to" some
influential program entity; or as retaliation for company or
personal reasons.

Many adverse ramifications result from giving exclusives.
Other broadcasters often react by boycotting the manu-

facturer who gives them. This results in a temporary air play ban on all of that company's products. Artists suffer from lack of air play. Their sales are crippled, which results in royalty losses. Writers and publishers lose broadcast performances and mechanical sales and ultimately, the manufacturer himself is negatively affected. Exclusive practices usually leave a feeling of bad taste and mistrust which is often irrevocable and has a disasterous effect upon the possibility of future air play. An atmosphere of distrust always surrounds the promotional guys that are suspected of giving exclusives. When promotional representatives are accused of giving exclusives, they naturally feign innocence. They are wide-eyed with disbelief that anyone could conceivably doubt their business virginity.

In the industry, promotion men are referred to as "heavyweights" or "lightweights." Heavyweights are the guys who break records. Lightweights don't break records. Heavyweights are made out of unknown quantities of layola, payola, groveling, entertaining, account overloading, request falsifying, dealer bribing, chart manipulation, job threatening, outside help, bullshit, special favors, list hyping, double dealing, talent and luck. Lightweights are made out of unknown quantities of layola, payola, groveling, entertaining, account overloading, request falsifying, dealer bribing, chart manipulation, job threatening, outside help, bullshit, special favors, list hyping, double dealing, talent and *bad* luck.

Every promotion man is "a heavyweight in his own right." Like, I'm a great brain surgeon in my own right, too. All promotion men extoll their own virtues without hesitation. They will always tell you which records they "broke" and which they "broke" but were not credited for "breaking." They'll tell you all of the key jocks they are "next to" or "tight with" and from whom they can always "get a favor when they need it."

Independent promoters handle many labels. Their prices vary, depending upon the market and the assignment. Some guys make up to fifty thousand dollars a year for their services. Many major record companies supplement their own full-time promotional staff with independents due to their specific talents to "get next to" certain broadcasters. Also, it's cleaner to hand out payola through independents, because it gets the unsavory contact outside of the corporation. Some independents are on lucrative manufacturer retainers for considerable duration. In these cases, their specific abilities are "tied up" to minimize competitive usage. Twenty thousand dollar retainers are not uncommon.

Promotional types spill across the industry like sour cream. They live in a world of ego and insecurity, clinging day to day to the whims and demands of a fickle broadcast empire and a childishly directed record industry. A sorry lot of guys, all dressed up, going nowhere, living from hit to hit.

4
Booze, Broads and Bagmen

I believe that the term T.C.B. was born in the recording industry. It means "taking care of business." The real impact of the expression never really shook me until I felt the devastating effects of it in practice.

Back in the spring of 1959, I had just been promoted to the position of Branch Sales Manager. My responsibilities were widened and I was viewing the future as a budding record executive. In fact, I bought two new Brooks Brothers cord suits to celebrate my entry into the attaché army.

Previous to my promotion, I had been a local salesman responsible for servicing retail accounts and radio stations within a prescribed territorial boundary. My field experience was broad and embraced every area of sales-promotional marketing. So, the business and I were no strangers. I was aware of its dishonesties and inconsistencies, but the total realization of payola's magnitude didn't hit me until my first actual confrontation with it early in 1959.

At this time, my company was employing a minimum of promotional specialists—people who called upon and serviced radio stations exclusively. So, the bulk of the promotional duties were absorbed by the sales personnel. My salesmen did a good job with radio outlets and my association with the programmers in my territory was excellent. In fact, I always enjoyed the promotional challenge and I prided myself in my ability to obtain air play for my product.

With the advent of independent label hits and the subsequent emergence of rock radio came great competitive pressures for air play from dozens of new companies. Product was being recorded and released by every guy who could pick a guitar and raise money for pressings. Labels were cropping up like weeds. Major label organizations were, for the first time, finding it difficult to get certain exposure for their merchandise. Mine was no exception. My company didn't openly condone payola, and the pressures were building. Competition was getting tougher. The business was growing and the insidious elements of gangsterism were budding in proportion.

A good friend of mine who was a musician was leaving to take a high-level job with a new recording entity. It was a Southwestern-based company that was enjoying good initial acceptance of its records. The company had offered my friend a huge salary inducement to leave his musician's post. Now I knew Jan was a good drummer, but for the life of me, I couldn't understand why any record company would want to offer such a whopping salary to a neophyte to the business of record marketing. Usually, the manufacturer looks for seasoned people who have a diversified background in the areas of sales, promotion and merchandising, but not in Jan's case. They were offering him a fantastic salary, unlimited expenses and the position of National Promotion Manager. Most people who achieve the rank of "national" anything in the record business, have at least some background and experience in the artistry of industry larceny and prevarication. Not Jan—just a nice little, music type with a good personality. But personality couldn't be enough. His company had to see some root advantage in hiring him that, for the life of me, I couldn't discern.

Well, anyway, Jan got the position. His standard of living bloomed. He sold his old Ford and picked up a new Caddie. His wardrobe suddenly took on the dapper record-business look of contrived "hip" and he even sprung for new glasses (no doubt more magnification so he wouldn't miss any zeros on his paycheck). He traveled constantly in his new role and his val-pack was dotted with stickers from the best digs in the nation.

During this period, I was also committed to a reasonable amount of air travel, due to the sizeable geography of my management domain. Jan was still headquartered in town also, so we flew together frequently and on many occasions traveled together when our routings coincided. Jan was an affable, charming road companion—always "up" and in cheery spirits. His suits were as bright as his demeanor, and he invariably carried a tightly rolled umbrella in one hand and a little black bag in the other.

Being intimate travelers, we naturally discussed records, artists, trends and other business aspects and Jan openly discussed every subject except his relations with the radio personnel he serviced. He never discussed program directors, music directors or disk jockeys. On the subject, he was mute, and this was unusual in a business where programmers are primary conversational delicacies. Another queer thing; as close as we had become, he would never make joint station calls or socialize while we visited in distant markets. After our flights terminated, he would mystically fade away to materialize next day at flight time. There he'd be—at the gate, smiling, holding his tightly-rolled umbrella and his little black bag. We exchanged products often. I'd give him samples of my new releases and he'd reciprocate. His company's stuff wasn't bad, but neither was my company's. Comparatively, I felt that much of my product had all the commercial appeal of Jan's. The relative air play, however, couldn't be compared. Jan's product was getting the hell played out of it, while much of mine, which I thought was equally as commercial, didn't get a smell. His product was being played like mad and it was retailing and his company was enjoying tremendous growth. Still, I couldn't reconcile the amount of air play he received. Jesus, here was a former small-time jazz drummer with no previous record business experience, getting fantastic results. It was hard to figure.

As I mentioned, Jan and I would always split company after deplaning. He'd go his way, I'd go mine. I never knew where he went, where he stayed, what he did. One night, though, chance negotiated a meeting. I was checking into a Pittsburgh Hotel when the desk clerk said: "Hey! Another record-guy just checked in a few minutes ago. In fact, he's in 1204—right down the hall from you."

"Oh, yeh! Really? Who is it?"

"Jan Johnson," he answered.

I was pleased to learn that Jan was a neighbor. Perhaps we could have dinner and bullshit around the city, I thought. After I checked in, I dumped my baggage in my room and wandered down the hall to 1204. I knocked on the door—nothing. I knocked again—still no response, but someone had to be in the room because the sound of voices was evident. In fact, all kinds of laughing and screaming party sounds were exploding inside the room. I tried the door and it was open, so I cautiously opened it and stuck my head inside. It was a suite. The sonofabitch had a suite. Immediately to my left was a bathroom which was off the entrance hall to the main room. On the front of the bathroom door was a full-length vanity mirror, and from where I was standing, I could see the reflection of the interior accommodations. Jan was sitting on a coffee table. He had a drink in his hand. He was laughing and he was nude. Across from him were two local radio personalities. They, too, were jaybirds. They were all drinking and laughing and making strange gestures with all the abandon of conventionaires. I poked my head in a little further. Now I could see what was motivating the revelry. On the floor near the end of the couch were two nude girls—one was black—one was white. They were making love. They looked like a couple of those scottie dog magnets—drawn together in feverish embrace. The guys were sitting there like spectators at a cock fight—cheering and applauding and rooting as if there were bets down on the first one to come. As I withdrew myself to make a quiet exit, my eye caught a glimpse of something else. On top of an end table was Jan's constant companion, the little black bag. It was open. Inside was money—mountains of fresh green cash. I knew then why Jan was getting such heavy air play.

Jan Johnson was what is commonly referred to in the business as "a bagman." He "took care of business." His company hired him, not for his capabilities as a record executive, but as a footman to buy air play with cash and women. His personality and his musical background made him a perfect choice for the role. Johnson was a "bagman" for years for his company. He traveled the nation, giving out money and "taking care of business." He played his part well. It is one of the key reasons his company has evolved into one of our major recording powers.

One of the most notorious bagmen to ever pay and lay for play worked for a major manufacturer out of New York City. We'll call him "Big Stan Blob." I remember with carnal clarity Big Stan's visits to Miami. Big Stan would always line up his gals preceding his visits to the city like an advance man for sin. All the programmers that could "do him some good" were notified. The hookers were hired. Food and booze was ordered and accommodations cleared well in advance of Mr. Blob's arrival. Nothing was left to chance at Big Stan's catered orgies.

Stan always checked into the Pharoah Motel in Miami Beach. It was his sex center and it fitted the part. The Pharoah was what I call "Early King Farouk." Everything stupendously overstated in a Vegas type recreation of a desert oasis. The place reeked with the phony tapestry that only bad taste could buy. (In fact, it just reeked!) The main dining room was like a juke box of the Nile—colored fans undulated in an air-conditioned monsoon—waitresses wore tiger-skin leotards—the waiters were costumed as shieks. The desert effect was carried throughout the joint. The bar was "the watering hole" and the background system spilled forth music that sounded like the soundtrack from Gunga Din. I never could fathom why camel pee was precluded from the drink menu. The swimming pool was surrounded by paper palms full of hanging paper monkeys with paper balls, and I hear that when the moon is full in Miami skies, and the oil tankers blow their horns out on the Atlantic, the Pharoah bartender burns tana leaves in a Pilsner beer glass and evokes a faggot mummy.

When Big Stan checked in, he always checked in "heavy." Never "light." Heavy with money and grass. He was always prepared, Big Stan, to take care of business in order to obtain air play.

Big Stan's orgies were of all-night duration. Guests would start arriving as early as 5 p.m. to enjoy the food, drink and women. Two rooms were taken so that the hookers could entertain the boys in private if they were bashful. If not, any and all acts were performed openly before the guests and most of the disc jockeys preferred an audience. Apparently, this gave full satisfaction to their exhibitionist tendencies. Bars were set up on top of dressers, nightstands and coffee tables. Plenty of the best quality booze and mix was available. Grass was in the prevailing wind also, and the musty smell bathed the atmosphere as joints were passed about casually. Food was available from bountiful buffets and room service calls were permitted to summon specialties.

The hookers worked constantly. One wondered what kept them so fresh and vital. They would consent to any act—no matter how perverse. One program director demanded that he be covered with instant whipped cream. Without hesitation, Big Stan special-ordered a carton of the stuff. The girls encased the guy in the fluffy mixture, then proceeded to eat away the milky garment. Wonderful fun for the whole family.

On a particular occasion, the local "important" disc jockey showed up with his two girl friends. He always had two girl friends. It was his badge of superiority and masculinity. His tribute to himself for being so accepted, so "big" in the market. His ego demanded that he be accompanied by a sexy duo, and the girls were sexy in the basest sense. They looked like they modeled for the covers of detective magazines. You know, big cleavage pushed up to look like water wings—wearing black hose and springalator shoes with sparkly glass heels. Real class! A true representation of what the industry had become.

When the disc jockey and his mattress backed book ends arrived, the payolafest was in full swing. The hookers were earning their wages with the efficiency of programmed wind-up dolls. Guests were cavorting like salivating dogs turned loose in a meat cooler, and Big Stan was presiding over the melee with the majesty of an inflated turd. Then, the "big disc jockey" plopped down cross-legged in the middle of this expanding madness and summoned his witless entourage to bring him food and drink. After sufficiently gorging himself, he instructed his girls to disrobe. Without hesitation, they began a strip-tease. Their undergarments were black and provocative and dripping with peep show cheapness. When they were naked, the jockey began to direct them in a spontaneous series of sexual improvisations.

First, he ordered a sexual display between the two girls. Then a mass flesh bath between the girls and the two hookers. These acts were supervised in detail by the disc jockey. He motivated and indicated moves and positions with the thoroughness of a major studio director. Each and every detail was overseen with stern concentration, which evoked new vistas of multisexual expression. When the girls finally unwound their mingled sweaty bodies, their commander ordered the cuties to copulate all the male guests. The girls began the rounds as if spirited by a magi. The sounds of flies being unzipped rose like the roar of a passing bomber squadron. Cries of ecstasy and laughter filled the smoky quarters and the din of unrestricted overindulgence swelled on the rising currents of corruption.

Payola practices are common in the entertainment industry. Publishers, record people at all levels—managers and artists, offer inducements, either overtly or subtly, to garner special air play considerations. Payola has been a key factor in the establishment of major artists, the evolution of publishing dynasties and the creation of recording empires. Payola, layola and taking care of business are the ABC's of the music industry past and present. It has taken many forms, and many publishers, artists, managers and record people at all levels have participated in payola practices.

One representative of a major publishing house used to prime air play with gifts. He made two road trips annually, covering the major marketing areas across the country. He always came loaded with baubles and trinkets, like a visiting maharajah. His briefcase warehoused French perfume, bracelets, watches, tie clips, brooches, earrings and a horde of other shiny ornaments. Some of the jewelry was grossly pornographic—little gimcracks like "fornicating lover cuff links" were popular items with the radio gang, so the representative always had an ample supply hidden in a concealed area of his portable hardware display case.

Another popular pay-for-play device was fly-ola. Airline tickets were purchased by the manufacturer or his representative. Several methods were used. For a short flight, the local promotional representative usually paid cash and obtained expense account reimbursement. For long-distance hauls, national moneys were used and costs were buried in some unrelated account or the tickets were purchased under a fictitious name and mailed to the broadcaster with instructions for him to fly under the pseudonym. Frequently, record personnel would purchase long-distance trips with their air travel card and the broadcasters would fly under the purchaser's name. When parties were knowingly under suspicion for payola, they used foreign-intrigue cunning rather than risk personal-transfer contacts and ticket mailings. In such cases, when an industry representative was departing a local air terminal, he would pruchase the broadcaster's ticket with cash or his air travel card. He would then deposit the ticket in a terminal luggage locker, and mail the locker key to the broadcaster. In this way, all incriminating contacts were neutralized.

I believe that fly-ola reached a pinnacle of absurdity when a record executive of my acquaintance made a prominent disc jockey the beneficiary to his airline insurance. A practice that I labeled "crash-ola."

Payola became manifest in many ways. Clothing bills were paid, rents absorbed, car payments were made and running night-club and restaurant tabs were paid directly by manufacturers. Vacations were underwritten, automobiles were purchased. I knew disc jockeys and program directors whose salary was two hundred per week, who drove Cadillacs and Lincolns, dined out nightly, vacationed at the nation's most posh resorts and dressed like Adolph Menjou. They were living just like the whores who were paid to ball them. Harlots, prostituting the tastes of musical America.

One disc jockey-program director loved to engage in any act of sex at any time, and the record pimps supplied his ravenous appetite. Once, while this guy was filling in for a vacationing all-night disc jockey, a well-known recording artist, sent a one hundred dollar hooker to the studio. The disc jockey was obviously blinded by the senuous slut, for he attacked her like a madman, apparently unconscious of the fact that I was looking on through the control-room window. Off went her clothes, off went his clothes. He laid her back against the master control board and began screwing her at 78 rpm. Every two or three minutes, he would have to stop to cue up disks, inject commercials, announce records and deliver his patter.

"Hello, guys and gals, friends and pals. . . . This is Big Boss Billy, right here 'til 5 A.M. filling in for Rancid Red Smith. Stay tuned because I'll be playing all the Fab 40, right through 'til dawn. And tonight, I'll be saluting all the kids out at Hallowed High School."

He'd close the mike, then renew his delights. The control board counter was bouncing and at one point, the needle came off the record being broadcast. The pace was hot and heavy. I expected the windows to begin to steam from the emotional outpourings, but they didn't and I was a privileged spectator to a scene that was both repulsive and humorous. Announcements for the heart fund were followed by animalism. Pleas for attendance at the church of your choice were followed by two undulating masses teetering on the edge of the control panel. At one point, the jockey assaulted the hooker atop his announcer stool. The stool was on casters and when he plunged into her with a well directed frontal attack, it went flying across the control room floor with the hooker on board. The chair and flailing occupant careened off of the soundproofed wall and the hooker fell flat on her rear with a smack that resounded through the insulated glass partition. I thought for certain that she had literally broken her ass, but evidently she was accustomed to such punishment for she displayed no signs of agony as the crazed jockey fell on top of her with the agility and pursuit of a tiger shark. A night-and-a-half to remember!

All payola proceedings do not follow the blatant course. Cash and hookers are the obvious inducements the manufacturers give to ply the airwaves, but there are other methods more subtle and infinitely more insidious.

The expense-account tool is the most common every-day payola vehicle. It is also most difficult, if not impossible, to draw definite payola conclusions from its usage. It's an ambiguous document that today is malleable in the hands of big business enterprise. As originally intended, the expense account was a necessary instrument. It was meant to absorb the expenditures necessary to the maintenance of normal business activities. Today it is just another cog in the corroded American big business machine.

Record industry people are notorious expense-account misusers, and the broadcasters take full advantage of their corporate generosity. And why shouldn't they? After all, they're in control. They know that air exposure is the lifeline to record sales. They know they have the record industry over the proverbial barrel, so it's "look out, Diner's Club, here we come." The record manufacturers representatives are constantly scrambling for broadcast acceptance and favoritism. Their life is on the line. Their future's at stake. One little favor, one little break from a broadcaster justifies their total being. So they sit cowering—insipid creatures, immobilized by a broadcast empire that doesn't really give a shit about them or their company. So they spend and buy and kiss ass. Half men—half servants.

Expense-account spending is rampant in the industry-broadcast romance. Lunches are cornucopias of food and drink. Dinners are feasts that rival the orgies of the Roman court. And the same broadcasters stuff themselves at the same restaurants—guests of the same industry agents, day after day, night after night, week after week—flaming this— and garnished that, sparkling vintage wines, hors d'oeuvre delights and dessert trays glistening with caloric splendor are consumed with bare-fingered gluttony, and the poetic hilarity is that the record industry never says no. They just keep pumping out the bread and dancing like jesters to obtain the little bones that the broadcasters occasionally spit at their feet.

Another way the manufacturers gain broadcast favors is through expenditures of advertising dollars. To exploit new album releases, the companies frequently purchase sixty-second spot announcements from the format stations. Spots are purchased in "flights" which are packages or groups of spots to be broadcast within limited chronological periods. For example, a "weekend flight" would simply mean that all spots would be aired between Friday evening and Sunday midnight. Manufacturers particularly like weekend buys due to the higher ratio of youth audience. Also constricting spots to run with consistency over a short duration creates a barrage effect that will hopefully motivate consumer acceptance through brain-washing.

The record companies have ample dollars budgeted for radio advertising. One million per annum is not uncommon. This budget is parceled out for buys at major market AM radio stations, the same markets, naturally, that are polled by the major trade publications. Now, even though a great portion of the time is purchased by record companies at the national or home office levels, particular care is taken to avoid bypassing the local promotional and sales distributing personnel. The manufacturer wants as much purchasing power in the hands of the local people as possible. Can you guess why? Well, here's why:

Local people are constantly in personal contact with the station's broadcast personnel and they need the benefit of any weapons that will help them combat programming resistance. Hopefully, if the programming staff is aware that the local distributing arm has available mass advertising monies, more air play will accrue to the distributor's product. Local promotion men with authority to trigger time-buys are more readily accepted by a radio station than a guy who just sits in the lobby with a stack of records waiting to buy lunch and eat crap.

Pressure for air play commensurate with advertising outlays is omnipresent throughout the industry. National offices are ritualistically demanding that their distributing agents "get some goddamned air play for that money we're spending with those bastards." And when a particular record is not added to a programming list or fares poorly at a station where spots are being purchased, the dictate to the field troops is: "Tell them fuckers if they don't play the record, we'll cancel the time buys."

There is constant behind-the-scenes maneuvering between station sales and programming and industry sales and promotion. Everybody is angling and conniving and lying and manipulating to "do right by all concerned." The radio sales boys and the promotional wizards join forces against the program department. The promotion man either begs or threatens the station sales executives, and the sales people, in turn, agree to put pressure on their programming departments. Naturally, station management emphatically denies that advertising pressures ever affect their programming decisions. They react with indignation to such suggestions and claim total, pure departmental divisions. Self-righteous clichés such as "one hand does not wash the other" support their airs of contrived shock.

Manufacturers also deny that they could ever sink so low as to utilize an advertising wedge. It's a travesty—a joke—the way everyone shrinks into their godlike cocoons—when, in the troubled waters of suspicion, everybody on all levels, on both sides, shrouds themselves in murky, black innocence, and like giant squids, slither off into the depths of management unknowns.

I was conceivably the first promotion man ever to be vested with substantial advertising authority. I knew the potentials to be realized from controlling radio advertising dollars at field levels and I had convinced my national management to permit me to administrate such funds within my territory. They agreed to the experiment and the results where phenomenal. No longer was I just a promotion man with a stack of "wax" and credit cards. Suddenly, I represented business. I controlled thousands of dollars of advertising money. My stock rose with the stations I serviced. Receptionists were more cordial. Sales managers, account executives and, yes, even station managers, were now back-bending with toothy amenities. Program managers, music directors and jockeys also began to relate to me on a new level. Now I represented dollars. I was big business.

My talk bristled with agency jargon. I spat "time buys," "flights," "avails," "packages," "Ros's," "down and unders," "billboards," "frequencies," and "impressions" with all the confidence of a Madison Avenue mossback. I was beginning to speak with tweed tongue.

The spot radio advertising was effective. It was beginning

to pay off in increased sales of the items ballyhooed. My firm increased my advertising allowance and expanded my authority over greater geographic territory. I was now the primary instrument that controlled spot campaigns and purchasing in a five-state area. Everything was going smoothly. Sales in my area were booming and air play was excellent. Seldom did I have to hassle programmers for air play.

One incident, involving one of my promotional competitors who was also vested with purchasing power, proved the influence of the advertising dollar. His company had just released a record by one of its biggest stars. It was an excellent record and it followed a long line of Top-10 performances by the artist. Normally, a programmer would add this record to the play list immediately, without question. Most of his stations had already "gone on" the record. One very important radio outlet in his territory, however, had "gone on" a competitive version of the song and he couldn't believe it. He was livid, furious.

Upon learning of this ridiculous competitive situation, he hopped a plane at once for the distant market. He arrived at the station early that afternoon, still bursting with anger. After all, losing air play through a competitor would reflect dimly upon his promotional credibility.

Now, the station in question was the beneficiary of a big chunk of his advertising budget. It was a top station with solid rating and he bought costly campaigns there nearly every week. During the preceding twelve months, he estimated that his purchases amounted to approximately sixty thousand dollars and what was he getting for it? The shaft, that's what. The ungrateful bastards were playing a competitive record by an unknown artist on a label that didn't spend a penny on their station. Enraged, he called a meeting between the program manager, sales manager and account executive. Once behind closed doors, he let go with a laser of invectives. How could they—these miserable, ungrateful creeps—turn against such a sponsor? After all, hadn't they by their acts of silence agreed to his many requests for programming "breaks"? He rambled on, condemning and cursing. Finally, he threw the big blow. He said, if they didn't cease playing the competitive piece of crap within one-half hour, he'd cancel all advertising present and future. Never again, would his company ever spend a rotten red cent, ever. Suddenly he could see that the spirit of sixty thousand dollars was descending like a bucket of slimy reality over their vacuous brains. They were shaken. He stormed out of the room and chaired himself defiantly in the reception area. Exactly, thirty minutes later, he was told by the program manager that the competitive version had been dropped in favor of his record.

Many jockeys are paid off with products. This product is called "freebies." The manufacturers deliver large quantities of records and albums to the disc jockeys who, in turn, peddle the merchandise through fences (particular dealers, one-stops and rack shoppers). Freebies goods must be disposed of at a fraction of their cost prices, and, therefore, great quantities have to be supplied in order for the seller to realize any substantial take. This is a very common practice and is perpetuated throughout the industry daily.

Freebies goods are written off as "promotional" merchandise and no artists, writers and publishing royalties are paid on product that is given away for promotional purposes. Also freebies usually consist of the best sellers—the cream—not necessarily selections that are being programmed as a result of the payola. Therefore, the name and "hot" artists are being unfairly penalized because they are being robbed to pay for air play for other artists' records. These freebies payola practices are of runaway proportions and amount to hundreds of thousands of dollars in royalty losses to artists, writers and publishers, and manufacturers lose fortunes due to lost sales.

Promotional bonuses and contests are also wily means of avoiding traceable payola connections. Manufacturers usually give special awards for specific air play achievements. For example, for getting a record added to a radio station play list, a promoter could be awarded one hundred dollars. If the record showed successive incremental chart gains at the station, he could be awarded additional bonuses for its growth—say fifty more if the record reached the Top 20. Fifty dollars again, if the selection climbed to Top 10 and another one hundred if the disk attained the lofty Number 1 spot on the station's Top 40 listings. In this example, the promotion representative would have received a total three hundred dollars for his achievement, and mind you, this three hundred dollars bonus applies only to the performance of one selection at only one radio station.

Some companies often pay as much as one thousand dollars as special merit awards. Monthly promotional bonuses in addition to base salary and expenses can be most rewarding. Two thousand dollars is not uncommon. The manufacturers pay well for air play.

The crafty promotion man uses his contest earnings and bonus payment system to garner more air play. He simply works out a kickback agreement with his programmers. It's simple: The programmer is the promotional representative's partner in the business of air play and the more play—the more pay. I knew a guy who was a promotion man in the

Southwest who won an impressive promotion by obtaining play by this method. His air play impelled gigantic bonuses which some months exceeded three thousand dollars, and he was kicking back fifteen hundred dollars in tax-free payola. His home office was so favorably impressed by his apparent promotional "talents" that they elevated him to a position of national scope and responsibility and another dishonest incompetent joined the ranks of many other recording executives who had also received their status through similar dubious achievements.

In many instances, the national promotional director authorizes phony bonus payments to cover his and his subordinates' payola commitments. From the national level, he frequently works out payola business by phone. He will then contact his local representative and update him relative to the deal. He then issues a special "bonus" check to the local man, who in turn cashes it and delivers the cash to the nefarious broadcaster. Other times, the local representative will indicate that he can buy air play and will request one of the "bonuses" to assure the exposure of a particular record. If the national man approves, and he usually does, a check is issued and the same cashing and delivering ensues. Tax burdens that are residual to the local promotional individual are recouped through authorized expense-account additions.

Programmers obviously must exercise extreme caution to avoid any obvious payola associations. Not only would payola involvements result in their dismissal and lay them bare for tax evasion, it would also inflict serious damage upon their employers. Stations would be tainted publicly and FCC license revocations could result. So the broadcast boys are foxy, crafty and coy.

Payola is still the industry's little bastard. No one will

admit to him, but everyone pays child support, and the little devil keeps coming back for more—not openly, of course— but quietly in sneakers. The greedy little bloodsucker has gone underground.

Yes, payola is still with us—part of the day-to-day business of doing business. It buys hits and creates empires and gnaws away at the fibers of decency.

Payola methods are wide and varied, and the subtleties employed to feed this cancer are among the industry's more creative works. If only a grain of the artfulness applied to the perpetuation of payola was converted to positive acts, the record companies would begin to experience rejuvenation rising out of self-respect.

5
The Bandwagon

Rodney Styvesant stood in the gardens of his family's palatial Back Bay estate. He was immaculate in his snappy blue crested blazer, white sailcloth trousers and snow-white Top-Sider Tennies. Around him the grounds were radiant with flowers and shrubs, and the bright morning sun gave the colors a depth and tonality that was boldly three dimensional. A hummingbird was vibrating from hollyhock to hollyhock, and its low hum gave a certain sense of electricity to the scene. Below him, behind a long sticky hedge, Rodney could hear the efforts of a tennis match in progress. He heard the ball as it met the "sweet" of the racquet with resounding twangs; he heard the tennis sneakers squeak as they made their adrupt stops on the court surface. It was a beautiful clean day, Rodney thought. It was crisp and invigorating here in Back Bay.

But in spite of his surroundings, his wealth, his apparent good looks, Rodney Styvesant was unhappy, unfulfilled. There was something missing; something intrinsically missing. Deep inside, he knew that his life, his wealth and position, were not enough. He felt isolated, removed from the true earth problems and the human plight of the real world, the mass world of pain and suffering. He, too, must suffer. He, too, must experience the anguish of the blues. Yes, the blues; the plaintive musical outcries of the true crippled world.

On this day, Rodney Styvesant made a decision. He decided to shake the coil of his Back Bay complacency and become an involved person in the real problems of the real world. He would become a country boy rock-and-roll singer and preach the gospel of the blues.

Rodney traded his Back Bay existence for an apartment in the East Village of New York City. The apartment was shabby and poorly heated. It was furnished with torn and shattered remnants that reeked with the stench of mildew and decay. A far cry from the sunlit gardens of Back Bay, but Rodney Styvesant liked it because it brought him closer to the real world of hunger and agony. It was the perfect setting—the perfect atmosphere in which he could assimilate the suffering of the actual painful world, and it supplied the solitude where he could practice his twelve string accoustic guitar and write his laments to the sad state of human existence.

And Rodney Styvesant practiced dilegently. For hours, days, he studied chords and fingering techniques. For seemingly endless periods, he played and wrote and sang. Only on Sundays would he drive his metallic, silver Rolls Royce up along the Hudson river. Slowly a new feeling began to well within him. He was getting it. He was starting to identify with the real world fraught with real torment. Rodney Styvesant was becoming a country boy rock-and-roll singer. He now felt the blues.

Rodney Styvesant took a job in a seedy village club. He hated clubs because they were in business to make money and to drain the real people of the agonized world, but he accepted the engagement in spite of this, knowing he must, in order to project his blues to the real people who were suffering. And the real people came and listened and nodded and were impressed. The word soon spread about this humble country boy rock-and-roll singer. Crowds came and Rodney Styvesant's reputation began to grow.

One night, representatives of a large recording corporation came to listen. They were impressed and they offered Rodney Styvesant a lucrative recording contract. Now, Rodney Styvesant hated recording companies, for he knew that they were greedy business men who exploited talent and deceived the poor huddled, oppressed people of the real world. But, he signed the contract anyway, because after all, how else could he reach the real, honest world masses of the country?

Now, Rodney Styvesant's recordings sold briskly, and the sales created a great growing wave of popularity that catapulted him to the level of super star. Yes, Rodney Styvesant was now a country boy rock-and-roll super star. Suddenly, he was forced to play the top clubs, which he hated because they were corrupt users of the real people. He stayed in the best hotels and ate the finest cuisine, which he also hated because it was not the fare of the suffering, distressed, real, honest people. He hated his bookers; he hated the press; he hated his record company; he hated his metallic silver Rolls Royce; he hated the police; he hated the government, and rightly so, because they were the oppressors of the real people—the migrants, the workers, the Appalachian Mountain forgotten masses.

And Rodney Styvesant kept on hating and singing the blues and making money. He hated the money, but he accepted it because it was his way of getting back at the businessmen he hated so much. So he kept on singing and making money he hated, and the poor, huddled masses paid ten dollars a ticket to see and hear their country boy rock-and-roll hero, and they bought his albums by the millions. And Rodney Styvesant hated the fact that his concerts were overpriced and that his record company charged so much for his albums. He knew they were greedy capitalists exploiting the real people of the actual, honest rural world.

Rodney Styvesant purchased a private jet airplane. He truly hated the jet, but it was necessary if he was to communicate his gospel to the remote masses of real people. He was, this country boy rock-and-roll singer, a Messiah. He knew it because he felt the blues. He'd make the sacrifice. He'd paid his dues. So he preached to the Indians on Alcatraz and on the great hot plains of the American Southwest. He protested along with the Negroes in Huff, Watts and Harlem. He marched with the Chicanos through the ghettos of East Los Angeles and he sat with the distressed people of the Appalachian plateau in the rolling hills of Kentucky, West Virginia and Tennessee.

Today, Rodney Styvesant is famous, good-looking and wealthy, and between concerts, club dates and pilgrimages, he retires to his newly constructed mansion overlooking the Pacific. He often stands alone there, in his bib overalls, facing the wind-driven waves, thinking. He recalls Back Bay and his genteel upbringing. The gay crowds of starchy, husky boys and straight-haired horsey girls; the soft summers; the boats on the lake; and the dinners at the club. What a hypocritical life, he reflects. What a souless group of unreal people living plushly in an unreal world. He breathes deeply, justifiably proud.

Musical saviours are testimonials to industry trendism, and "country boys" crop up all over the record business. Today, country is "in." It's "heavy" and "where it's at." So, people become "country" artists in order to hitch a ride on the industry bandwagon.

Success stories start trends, and trends *are* the record business. Every new type of hit is heralded as the beginning of a new musical era. Every successful group sets a trend for the industry and the industry follows it, right down dead-end dollar alleys.

The "country" trend is a typical example of industry hysteria. Back in 1968, "The Band" emerged out of the "Big Pink" with a valid musical statement. Their musicianship was slick and the writing and performance valid; a good, solid work. The Bands' success prompted immediate industry spin-offs. Artists suddenly became "country." Rock acts converted. Country-style harmonies, mandolins, banjos and violins were exhumed to take an active part in the country revolution. Overnight, roots and rural were "in." Record executives began exhaustive searches for country-rock acts. Kids who'd spent their entire eighteen years in Manhattan, began to turn country. God, the country was turning country. Terms like "down home" and "laid back" evolved. And rock musicians began to refer to their girl friends as their "women." Attire also reflected the rural influence. Long underwear peeped from beneath plaid lumberjack shirts. Feet were laced into barnyard boots. Bib overalls reappeared as a sartorial winner and railroad handkerchiefs and caps were resurrected. Hay seeds and horse shit hit the image fan and were scattered to the winds. Another trend was born.

Record America is a trendy business. In fact, the industry looks for trends to follow because it's *not* a leader. It's a track record business, overflowing with cliché-popping, over-dressed people who bury new ideas and innovations. Anyone who tells you that the record industry is an avant-garde, sensitive organism of the arts is either completely mad or owns a publishing company. Record companies aren't creative. They're borax musical factories that grind out records and albums to oversaturate an already oversaturated market. If you don't believe me, visit any record manufacturer's headquarters. Your trip will be about as esthetic as a guided tour through a disposal plant.

Bandwagons, that's what the industry rides—bandwagons. Everybody on board wearing flared pants, flowered shirts and funny shoes, beating bass drums for yesterday.

The manufacturers, the trades, producers and artists are bandwagon people, creating and perpetuating trends. Success spurs imitations and the imitations, more imitators, and everybody imitates the imitators.

When a mellow vocal group succeeds, the industry goes on a "soft sound" kick. "Soft sounds are in," "soft sounds are back," "soft sounds sell." When a girl vocalist has a big hit, suddenly it's the "female era." "Girls are back," and on and on with big bands, single artists, baritones, Dixieland, country, soul, etc., etc.

Then there are the "rockisms," which are coined by the industry. "Country-Rock," "Rock-a-billy," "Jazz-Rock," "Rock-Art," "Dixie-Rock," "Soul-Rock," "Latin-Rock," "Jesus-Rock," "Afro-Cuban-Rock," "Chicken-Rock."

Of course, the blues is always "in," really "in." All of the record industry heavies are into the blues. They "know where the blues is at." What a laugh! What bandwagon bullshit nonsense. Most industry people and artists I've met wouldn't know the blues if it crawled into bed with them. But, they go around empathizing and expounding endlessly about roots and soul and the meaning of the blues. They go through all manner of histrionics about Blind Lemon and Lightin' Hopkins, Muddy Waters and Jimmy Reed to prove their knowledgeability on the subject. Hell, blues ain't knowledge; blues is feeling, and you don't get the feeling by putting patches on your ass and wearing shit-kickin' boots.

Industry boys are currently getting on the bandwagon with Jesus. Yes, Christ suddenly is big business. It's even been rumored that the "Jesus Christ Superstar" album is going to replace the Gideon bible in the hotel rooms of America.

Jesus Freaks all over the country, are beating out their rock gospels and the record industry's saying, "Amen, brother." "Jesus-Rock" is very "in," very contemporary. It's a trend, so look out, Moses. The Red Sea bit was kid stuff. Wait till you see what the record boys do with this one. And the artists are just as bad. Many of them, too, are rock crusaders for Christ. Overnight, they're off of grass and into the bullrushes.

Just the other day I had lunch with a rock drummer friend of mine. I'd just gotten my spoon into my onion soup, when he pulled a miniature bible on me. He began to read with evangelical passion. When he finished, I asked:

"Has it helped your playing any?"

"Absolutely," he replied.

"Then how come, you can't keep time?"

Yesterday is also big business, and the industry is dipping its mitts into the past. Repackaging of dated albums is in vogue to meet the current trend towards nostalgia. Old "gems" are being hauled out, given new titles and new covers. There's usually no royalties on this stuff, so the manufacturers really clean up the profits. Yes, yesterday is hot and the manufacturers are hot after the trend.

One of the saddest aspects of record industry trendism are the middle-age record men and artists who struggle to maintain "with it" youth images. These poor clods outfit themselves in costumes of circus proportions. One evening, I remember, one of the guys at Capitol left the building in his nice-looking grey, three-button suit with respectable center vent. He'd always dressed this way and he always looked very nice. Apparently, though, his age was gnawing at his guts, and he felt his image didn't say "record biz," because, the next morning, the guy showed up wearing white shoes with tiny gold side buckles, harlequin designed double-knit bell-bottom pants and a Cavalier-width belt. His shirt was white fluffy silk with billowy puffed sleeves; an orange patterned kerchief was knotted about his neck. He looked as if he was going to play in an accordian recital. And, this was just the beginning. Day after day, he draped himself more ridiculously.

Older artists often try to capture the youth image. I'm sure you've seen them on television wearing fringed vests, buckskin jackets, kerchiefs and sideburns; always, those goddamn wooly, grey sideburns, looking strangely like elephant tusks.

It's disheartening to see these people struggling to look like kids. They can't; it's impossible. All they do is succeed in making themselves up like fools; caricatures of youth.

Merchandising and advertising trends are also ubiquitous in the industry. Certain types of graphics and ad art are constantly emerging to be picked up and carried along by the industry imitators. Cartoon type album covers, showing artists names and album titles in thought balloons is big; fifties ad art is also a biggee; grainy blowups are good; sepia reproductions of "down home" family album portraits are hot; abstraction is always good; dada is great; cute double-meaning photos are fine; any shot of anyone lofting a clenched fist or giving "the finger" is super; religious motifs are in; nudity is neat and pornography is sensational.

Billboards sport all the hot trendy stuff. It's a contest to see who can "out-hip" who. Special effects are used; costly lighting applied and ingenious three dimensional feelings are created. Some of these billboards are gigantic and cost thousands, thousands of stupid bandwagon dollars that could be passed on to the consumer in the form of price savings. But who thinks of the consumer in the hop, skip and jump to "out-hip" the other guy in the trend game?

The "kindly little-old record company" trend is another slick piece of industry advertising. I'm sure you've seen the ads. They are obviously condescending. They employ all the "in" "hip" lingo in order to get to the kids and to show them that the kindly little-old record company is really aware. These ads utilize the "underplayed" angle to distasteful excesses; "right-ons" and "dudes" and "heavys" and "wows" and "rip offs" pop like corn in the industry advertising kettle. Quite often, ads even put down and ridicule the record business in order to get down to and inside the youth market—a real sweet, self-lowering job in an attempt to pick up consumer label loyalties.

Fab, groovy, geer radio spot advertising is another repulsive aspect of the industry's attempt to "get to the kids" on *their* level with *their* language. Really! The industry certainly *has* a low opinion of their potential consumer's intelligence, because the phony, contrived, overproduced stuff that they pour out is crass, insulting slurp; as example:

> Spot opens with music up. Spot drops down and under announcer's voice. Announcer's voice is smooth and intimate and dramatically sinister.
>
> "It's . . . it's 'cowshit.' " Music up for a few seconds; then music down and under announcer's voice.
>
> "Yes . . . it's 'cowshit,' erupting out of the bowels of rural America like an exploding apocalypse of sound . . . 'cowshit'"
>
> Music up again for few more seconds, then down.
>
> "Soil and sound are intermingled in a mosiac of root's truth in 'cowshit's' latest Bovine Records release. . . . On sale now! . . . 'Cowshit.' " Music up and out into fade.

The trend to minutely detailed album jacket liner notes exemplifies the length to which artists and record companies will go to perpetuate a "good thing." Liner notes are often more intricate than the music they house. Wordy explanations relative to musical personnel—engineers, producers and arrangers—are given; special thanks are awarded to various and sundry people—from in-laws to studio janitors. In fact, it's "very hip" to give credits to totally irrelevant individuals like girl friends, pals, cops, kindly old Bill the custodian who "brought in sandwiches," cleaning ladies, fathers and mothers, Gip the dog, "who kept us all laughing," instrument repairmen, road managers, Bill, Alice, Jocko, Mary, the Goodwin twins, copyists, errand boys, and Sam "who made it all possible."

Vast detail is also spent explaining away the hidden meaning of musical selections; instrumentation is delineated; inspirational writing motivation is dealt with in depth; lyrics are often reprinted in the author's own hand to lend a touch of authenticity to the mishmash. For the sound freaks, there are frequently mounds of drivel about microphone types, tape equipment, control boards, cutting heads, and other technical tripe; times, dates and places, are indicated, too, because apparently everyone is interested in knowing that "Side One–Cut One" was recorded on June 15, 1970, at the Golden Groan Studios in Upper Darby, Pennsylvania.

Recording studio trendism is another trade malady. Recording studios where artists, a group, anyone, has "cut a hit" becomes a Pantheon and artists flock to these temples of tape like lemmings. The artists believe deeply that, because a hit has been recorded at a particular facility, they, too, will emerge from its hallowed confines with a "million seller." Often, if an artist learns that a big hit had been cut at a certain studio, he will go to great trouble to superstitiously recreate the exact conditions for his recording date. He will hire the same engineer that the hit artist used; insist upon the same studio; demand the identical microphone and microphone setup; ask for the same recording hours; he will even attempt to determine the exact spot where the other artist stood. Somehow, someway, the artist believes that by reconstructing the scene, success will mysteriously rub off on him. He seldom considers the most important factor . . . TALENT.

Hit associations are gold mines for the recording studios who are lucky enough to fall beneficiary, and it *is* luck; it's talent and timing and tape–all unexplainably colliding cataclysmically when the moon is in proper phase. All the bunk about studio "sound" is real artistic bullshit, but the lucky studios capitalize. They install lavish control boards that glow ominously like giant outer-space pinball machines. They install special lighting to create special moods. They cover control rooms and studio floors with thick pile carpeting. Multitracking equipment is constantly updated to keep abreast of the competitive studio syndrome; eight, sixteen, twenty-four tracks are made available. A cascade of resistors, transistors, relays, cathodes, microphones, pods, timers, booms and V.S.O.s, phasers, filters, equalizers are outdated, upgraded, replaced and outdated, and the cost of recording soars, and the artists and the record companies throw away millions because they think technology makes hits.

Similar hysteria establishes production empires. Producers with "hit" track records are big gears in the industry trend mill, and the manufacturers and artists clamor for their services because they actually believe that these producers have the "golden touch"—the magic, genius granted by the grace of spiritual revelation—and the producers take advantage. They're "in" and they know it and they show it by escalating their prices and cracking stiff bargain whips.

"Regional genius" is the most current, chic, production trend. Nashville, Detroit, Memphis, Muscle Shoals are domestically "in." Europe, of course, is very "in" now, and, well, London . . . man, it's the "inest."

The guest-musician trend is also mighty hip. Rock stars are always popping up as guest performers on other artists' recording dates. It's a standard industry trick to install super stars as guest performers on relatively unknown artist's sessions; a merchandising ploy that's intended to sell more records and albums.

Dredging up old blues stars to record with rock artists is a going trend. Poor old, unsuspecting musicians are rounded up to "sit in" with the Contemporary Boys. It's "in," very hip and pitifully cruel, the way these forgotten giants are used to hypo sales. Living legends become living gimmicks in the ever-evolving trendism of the record biz, and the old blues kings just sit there on the bandwagon, strumming their banjos and smiling as the industry parade rolls on.

6
Where Did All the Royalties Go?

Industry contract people are always on the prowl for unsuspecting talented lambs; naive artists who will unwittingly sign slaveholder contracts and commit themselves to a musical Devil's Island. Since struggling talent is vulnerable and therefore easily flattered and misled, the chances of their hastily signing the fine print documents are great and the contract boys know this, so they importune graciously while twitching behind free-form desk tops.

Certainly, it's to a manufacturer's advantage to negotiate as many of these "vanilla" contract deals as possible. Low royalties, publishing tie-ups, long-haul options, record club cop-outs and freebie gimmicks are contractual panaceas for the corporation because they assure greater profit contributions as a result of minimized payouts. So, the funny little guys in the funny little suits with the sweaty handshakes and painted grins, are invariably looking for quick signatures.

Standard contracts are, it goes without saying, always written in the record company's favor. This is only natural, and I'm sure to some degree, justifiable in this day of rocketing costs and irrepressible egos (conditions, ironically, that the industry has created). But the number of hidden meanies and their ultimate damaging effects are gross injustices to star-struck, unknowing artists, who either can't afford legal counsel or trustingly, never consider retaining any.

Let's take a look at some of the hidden pitfalls that often are buried in a typical recording contract and how they punish artists and reward the negotiators.

An artist is asked to sell himself for a minimum initial period of one year plus options that can secure his talents for an additional six years. This means that the artist is potentially locked up for seven years. His recording activities are exclusively the company's for this period of time.

Most contracts indicate that the company is under no obligation to record or release the artist's material and that the company's only liability is to pay the artist minimum union scale for the number of selections stipulated in the contract. This means that the company, if it so chooses, can restrict the artist from recording for seven years so long as they pay him minimum union wages for the number of sides (musical selections) per the contract agreement. I personally know artists who have rotted on a lable due to this contractual provision. A friend of mine was contracted to a label for three years without having a record released. His company thought he had talent, so they held on to him. In fact, they even spent heavy session money to record him. They recorded fifteen sides with him, but never released a one. He used to joke disparingly that he was going to receive the "golden can award" for the most masters consigned to the vault. His company really held him up; literally ruined his career.

Standard contracts usually stipulate that artists do not accrue royalties on product that is utilized for promotional purposes. (Promotional merchandise is merchandise that is given to radio stations and reviewers and utilized for other legitimate, constructive promotions.) Unfortunately, for the artist, "legitimate" is a term unknown in the industry, and the manufacturers frequently, through indiscriminate over-promoting, give away excessive amounts of product; five thousand albums, for example, should assure adequate national promotional coverage. I've known many cases, however, where up to thirty thousand copies of an album selection were given away for all sorts of mailings, contests, and other idiotic gimmickry. Practices that clobbered corporate profits and artists' royalties.

Not too long ago, a manufacturer released an album by one of its best-selling artists. As expected, the consumer demand was immediate. The album took off like crazy. Suddenly, there was no warehouse stock to fill orders and backorders were mounting daily. Forecast people were baffled. They were positive that enough stock had been pressed to meet the expected initial demand. What had gone wrong? A quick inventory card analysis revealed the problem. So much stock had been given away that there was none left to sell.

Another contract stipulation is that all recording costs are recoverable from artists' royalties. That's right. Artists pay for their own recording sessions. Due to the outrageous cost of recording, it is conceivable that an artist can have a hit and not make a penny.

Say, an artist records six sides; the session costs (musicians, studio time, arranger, etc.) are $12,000. Okay? Now, the company releases two of the sides (a single record) and the record becomes a hit, selling 300,000 disks. At a royalty rate of 5 percent of 90 percent of all suggested retail price (which is 98¢), the artist will receive around $12,000. He makes nothing. He merely offsets the cost of recording. The manufacturer, on the other hand, scoops up big profit.

On any big hit, the manufacturer will begin realizing a profit shortly after release date (up to 50 percent gross margin). The artist, however, must wait until production costs are recouped before he can begin realizing royalty benefits.

Rock groups, in particular, get killed with studio costs due to the laborious nature of their session techniques. Layering, tracking, experimenting and mixing often takes days, weeks; $20,000, $50,000, $30,000, $80,000, $40,000 are normal session expenditures. I remember my own experience with The Misfits. One particular album cost us $18,000 to produce. When the royalty statement arrived, I cringed. The group dropped $18,000 and I lost a healthy management percentage. Costly productions over which artists frequently have no control, cost them thousands.

Standard contract terms always attempt to minimize royalty rates. Companies try to get away with 4 to 5 percent of 90 percent of suggested retail. Wise contract bargainers can always negotiate more favorable percentage terms. Eight percent is good, and 10 percent is terrific.

A quality magnifying lens exactingly applied to contract fine-print hieroglyphics will normally make discernable an innocent clause entitled "packaging allowance." Ambiguity is personified by this clause, which can allow the manufacturer to pick up extra revenues at artists' expense. Here's how they do it, the clever devils:

Stipulated contractual percentages are deducted from album list prices, then royalties are computed on the remaining figure. Let's assume, for example, that a manufacturer's "packaging allowance" is 20 percent. Royalties are computed as follows:

First, the 20 percent "packaging allowance" is deducted from the suggested album list price of, say, $5.98, leaving a figure of $4.78. The artist's royalties are then computed on 90 percent of $4.78. At a 7 percent royalty rate, the artist would recover 30¢ per album-unit sold.

In actuality, however, the album jacket may have cost the manufacturer only 15¢. A substantial royalty differential is obvious. At the actual 15¢ jacket cost, the artist would have recovered 37¢ per album retailed. The artist, in this case, loses 7¢ per album-sale.

Packaging allowances range from 6 percent to 20 percent. 15 percent is an average.

Another dipsy provision is that the manufacturers may dispose of surplus stock, catalog cutouts and deleted merchandise, as he so chooses, without sharing profit returns with anyone. The average album costs the manufacturer 50¢. They frequently liquidate them for from 75¢ to $1.50 per unit. The excess is theirs—all theirs.

"Dumps" are ofttimes damaging to artists whose regular sales are diluted due to the abundance of cheapy goods on the market; stuff that's selling in supermarkets, drug stores, syndicate stores and slop shops for 98¢, to $1.29, $1.49, etc. "Dumps" can also be most harmful to artists' images. Suddenly, the buying public relates to them as "budget artists" instead of first-line performers. And, remember, the artist doesn't get a sou for his items sold through "dump" deals.

Some contracts also provide for seamy record-club shenanigans. Record clubs are forever waving inducements to attract new memberships. There are always "giveaways." Free phonograph records and albums are offered to generate subscriptions. Album "freebies" are probably the most common attractors that are flagged in front of the American magazine reader to suck up new record-club members. "Free, Free Free," shouts the advertising, and why not? The record companies don't pay the artists royalties on freebies. The contracts assure this.

Contractual provisions often state that manufacturers will not pay royalties on "promotional freebies." Remember? So, the companies give the clubs merchandise to induce membership and create sales. The manufacturers, though, work out their own club deals without disclosure to the artists. All that the artists know about their club participation is that they will be paid a reduced rate of 50 percent of their regular royalties for record-club sales. Little do they know what goofy wheels are turning counterclockwise to their careers.

Club deals are usually written to benefit manufacturers and screw the artists, the big artists in particular. Here's how the fiscal fornicating works:

Major artist "A's" album is offered as a record-club selection. It is also offered as a free giveaway inducement to new club subscribers. Now, 100,000 albums are sold through membership selectivity and 200,000 are given away as new subscription inducements. The manufacturer/record-club agreement calls for the club to pay the manufacturer on 50 percent of the total movement, which in this example, is one-half of 300,000 or 150,000 sales. The manufacturer however, due to the "freebie" waiver clause in the artists contract, is only committed to pay the artist 50 percent of royalties on 100,000 albums. So, the manufacturer is paid on 150,000 albums; the artist on only 100,000 albums. Also, 200,000 of the artist's albums were given away free to entice new record-club subscriptions; 200,000 albums that conceivably could have been retailed through regular channels and could have returned royalties to the artist at full rates. What duplicity!

Another example of fiscal shafting is the stipulation that only 50 percent of royalties will be paid on tape sales. What complete audacity these record people possess to suggest the artist give up half of his royalties on lucrative tape sales. Cassettes, eight-track and reel-to-reel tape sales are huge, no longer just a stepchild to the record album. Tape sales often sell as much as 30 to 50 percent of their disk counterpart, which can amount to 100,000 to 250,000 unit sales relative to a hit album. Besides, the suggested list price for tape is greater than for albums, and therefore royalties are proportionately higher.

Provision for "reasonable reserves" is another contract trap that can ensnare the unsuspecting artist. "Reasonable reserves" is an arbitrary amount of accrued royalties that a manufacturer may withhold pending returns of artists' merchandise. Say, for instance, you're an artist and you have accumulated $100,000 in royalty revenue. Your manufacturer, if he wishes, can withhold a "reasonable" amount to guard against an unexpected flood of distributor returns of your records and albums. In other words, he is not willing to pay out fully on merchandise for which he hasn't been paid or for which he expects to issue credit due to lack of consumer sales. (In the record biz, most stock is sold on 100 percent exchange or return for credit privileges.) So, if he wishes, a manufacturer can hold back a "reasonable reserve" to cover such losses.

The question that arises here is what is "reasonable reserve" and what is a "reasonable" withholding period. The manufacturer could conceivably hold all of your royalties for five years under the shelter of "reasonableness." Usually, with major labels, reserves are minimal, but smaller manufacturers, often in deep financial troubles, hide behind the contract goody "reasonable reserve" when they're in fact maintaining their operation by functioning on the artist's money.

Manufacturers also always try to lock up new artists' publishing rights during the period of initial contract negotiations. All manner of sugary arguments are used to convince the artist that the company's publishing affiliate is the most heavyweight outfit in the industry. Talented writers can make millions for a publisher, and the manufacturers are well aware of the longevity potentials of valuable copyrights. So, they move swiftly to tie up all new artists to long-term writer's agreements.

There are many little meanies, lurking, rubbing their hands in the small-print jungles of many industry contracts.

I've only exposed some of the obvious ones. Hopefully, though, this will help some unsuspecting artist avoid the contractual quagmire where many are stuck, sinking up to their knees, up to their waists, up to their necks, and finally—glub! glub!

7
The Producers

Originally, the A & R (Artist and Repertoire) man was a staff employee who was responsible for an assigned stable of artists. His job was to select their musical material and to administrate and supervise their recording sessions. He was also counselor to his artists, overseeing their recording careers with parental guidance. His musicianship was of the first order. In fact, legitimate musical understanding was an A & R requisite and many of the earlier big-name A & R people were excellent musicians who had distinguished themselves as respected leaders and sidemen.

A & R leaders held lofty positions in their recording organizations. They were the musical musicians who craftily guided the careers of their company's most valuable assets— the artists. It was their job to develop viable recording careers that would have substantial corporate residual effects in the form of profits. So, these boys were respected. They were looked up to with a certain reverence. They were the talented, venerated gentlement of recordom.

The A & R man's relationship with his artists was usually one of mutual respect; respect for each other's professional craftmanship. Artists "went over" material with their A & R man. Artists were consulted, advised and guided. Joint musical decisions were made, based upon the artist's and the company's best long-range interests, and the artists believed in their A & R men and their company and its departmental operations. They were gentlemen who knew their trade and, therefore, felt secure that others knew theirs. But, this was before the record industry ran away with itself; before it began overreacting to trends, tastes and times. But, changes occurred and the predictable axis of consumerism shifted. Youth and radio and rock activated another cycle.

A few major record companies still maintain staff A & R people (now called staff producers), and some of the important early A & R staffers are still around doing special assignments for the major labels. But, by and large, the industry looks to the independent producers for its marketable material.

The independent-producer concept evolved essentially out of the independent record boom, when new labels were sprouting up anywhere, everywhere. Two guys, for instance, would get together in some garage studio facility in East Dubuque. They'd write, arrange, play and sing their own material. They'd go in the pocket for a couple of hundred dollars, and have a hundred copies of their record pressed on their own independent label. They were, of course, *their own* producers and they would credit themselves as such on their record label. The hundred pressings from this new record company would then be delivered to area radio outlets for possible play. If, miraculously, the selection obtained exposure and created a consumer stir, arrangements were made to sell this "master" to a large manufacturer with reputable distributor affiliations. Terms of the master purchase agreement assured the artists production rights for the period of the contract. New producers were born.

This is only one example, there are many variations. But this is essentially how the independent producer was born. How obscure artists, writers and investors in remote locations rose to dominate today's industry. Today's contemporary artists are largely self-contained. They compose and perform their own material. They produce their own sessions in studios of their own choice. Production control is no longer "in house." It is in the hands of artists, writers, and production companies. The manufacturer's role has become one of Big Daddy. He has become a buyer, packager and distributor. The artists and production outfits are contract performers who deliver finished works for industry marketing.

Multimillion-dollar corporations have been founded upon humble productions. In two cases, one record, for example, spirited the growth of Motown and A & M Records. One record, "Shop Around," gave Barry Gordy the impetus to build an empire. "Lonely Bull" structured the underpinnings for Herb Alpert and Jerry Moss's goldmine. A single production, talent and determination brought these struggling unknowns international prominance.

During the 60s the stature of the producer grew. In-house productions began to dwindle. Everybody was producing, forming record labels. New York, Chicago and Los Angeles were weakened as recording strongholds as other areas began to emerge as important entities. Memphis, Nashville, Muscle

Shoals were starting to absorb industry attention. Good studio facilities were now available or being built in every significant market, and hits were being cut everywhere. The industry master purchasing spree was causing record expansion. It was a seller's market and Big Daddy was buying. Everyone was producing. Kids with a hundred bucks were cutting in two-track basement studios. Successful producers were adding twelve strings and timpani, and production companies were grinding out finished goods for quick resale and profit gains. And Big Daddy kept buying and approving budgets and releasing more records by more producers than ever before. And if you had a "track record" you could retire for life.

A legitimate track record should evolve out of consistent, successful performances. However, in a business so ego-packed and fickle, one record can be your track record and your lifetime annuity. Producers with one or two hits have been known to parlay such "success" into substantial careers and have established themselves as industry "geniuses." The industry is notorious for sucking up pure, unadulterated bull. It's afraid of missing something, of passing on a hit.

So it was during the independent producer boom of the 60s. Everybody had a chance. The corporate dollars were ripe on the industry money tree and the opportunists picked away like itinerant farmers harvesting bountiful baskets of goodies with little risk and less talent. Producing became big business. Investors, con men and mobsters financed production companies. Many of these no-talent backers demanded label producers' credits, and if one of their "productions" hit, they were instantly established as industry heavyweights.

The record industry had by now created an inertia that

was unstoppable. Big deals and bad decisions were perpetuated by management teams that would have had difficulty running sno-cone wagons. A & R decisions were, and still are, made by individuals who usually achieve their important executive status as a result of their "track records." People who produced hits, discovered a hit act, put together "a string of winners," or personally knew a guy who knew Bob Dylan, were, and are, promoted into executive positions. Imagine, some guy, some nondescript bullshit artist, being elevated to the level of decision making, management and administration due to his ephemeral "creative" associations. Is he responsible? Does he understand marketing tenets? Can he handle people? Can he administrate budgets? Silly questions, seldom considered by an industry snowed by its own image.

Today, all the world's a producer. Every guy with a guitar is potential producer stock. I swear, everyone, everywhere is waiting, itching to get into a recording studio where he can emerge as a production giant. It's a particular industry malady. Salesmen, sales managers, promotion men, office file clerks, vice presidents, art directors, secretaries, plant foremen, mail clerks, controllers, time keepers, accountants, administrative assistants, personnel directors, engineers, press operators, merchandising staffs, publishers, publishers' representatives, receptionists, maintenance crews, janitorial help, and presidents all claim production prowess and are positive they know "how to pick them."

Today's independent producers and production companies negotiate substantial production deals with manufacturers. This allows them to operate on the lucrative corporate advances. Deals come easily for producers with track records, because after all, they produce hits and they're in demand

and manufacturers clamor for their services with typical industry recklessness, and the deals reflect the industry compulsiveness.

Today's successful independent producers, staff producers and production companies, not only make money via label deals, master sales and royalty overrides, they also maneuver in other ways to amass wealth and create corporate dynasties and individual demi-empires. A & R positions are unscrupulously used to rake off lucrative hidden money, and the skeletons are buried beautifully. For example:

Every A & R producer I've ever known maintains his own publishing company or companies and exercises every pressure to tie up the writing talents of the artists he records. In fact, this is usually provisional to the production or contract agreement. Well-known producers with track records are in demand. They are in positions of strength and are able to intimidate artists. So, they hold up artists for publishing rights, which could be their greatest long-range asset. When the artist signs over the publishing rights to his material, he automatically assures the publisher of an additional penny for every selection sold, and at least four cents more for every radio air play, not to mention revenues for sheet music, TV, movies, live performances and other recorded performances. He is also the copyright holder to a potentially golden piece of property and copyrights can be worth millions. (I believe that the song "Moon River" has already returned well over one million dollars.)

Staff producers, due to conflicts of interests, bury their publishing proprietorships by establishing operational fronts and using pseudonyms so that they, too, can pull off publishing dollars from the performances of many of their artists.

Let me give you an example of how a staff producer might approach a potential recording artist:

"Say, look. I think you have talent and I'd like to produce you. In fact, I've already spoken to our contracts people and if you can ease in this week, I think we can wrap the deal. Oh, by the way, I told them that you were already a contract writer for another publisher. So, if they ask you about it, just verify my story. Okay? Now, if you'll just sign this publishing agreement with my little company, we'll get things going."

Of course, the young, naive artist, fearful of losing a major recording contract is in no position to refuse. He will, usually, sign readily.

Producers also squeeze publishing firms for a piece of the action. If they are interested in recording material not in their domain, they will approach the outside publisher for a cut. First, they'll ask for a piece of the song and try to get a 50 percent copyright assignment. If this fails, they'll request a split on monies collected as a result of sales and performances generated specifically by their artist's rendition. If all fails, they'll either refuse to record the material, or, if they feel the material is supersensational, do it. But, in any case, the pressure is always applied and the squeeze is made to "get a piece."

Producers and production companies work on production budgets. That is, when a manufacturer contracts outside production work, or when a production deal is sold to a manufacturer, a recording budget must be submitted to and approved by the client. These budgets are almost always inflated, and the producers instigate patchworks of trickery to hold down their costs and increase their profits.

Producers and production companies almost always inflate

their projected recording budgets. This excess, if questioned, is explained away as payment for the producers artistic time and talents. This is normal bull and the industry swallows it with usual submission. After these water-logged budgets are approved, the production people hack away at subdeals and kickbacks. Frequently, recording studios are asked to give cut-rate prices, but to submit, however, bills indicating regular rates. Recording artists are asked to kick back their union wages for studio performances. I have known groups who have recorded for days, and who then turned back all of their American Federation of Musicians (AFM) earnings to their producers or production companies.

Side deals are also made with arrangers and contractors. Producers often convince arrangers to submit double arranging bills for subsequent splits and kickbacks. Contractors, are musicians who specialize in organizing musical personnel for recording dates. If, for example, a producer needs twelve strings, he will simply contact his contractor who will hire the personnel for the session. The contractor acts as a sort of musical middleman; a wholesaler, who eliminates a sizeable amount of busy work. He makes all the arrangements. Contractors are paid double the sessions scale for their involvement. Many producers "work with" their contractors and receive kickback splits.

Double billing, which I refer to as "stereo billing," is a regular producer ploy. Double studio bills are submitted; double AFM contracts; double conductor services; double instrument rental bills; double AFTRA contracts, and double arranging fees are entered. Let me give you a specific example of a double-billing kickback: A producer approaches a member of a group he is going to produce. He informs the musician that he's going to show him as "leader" on all AFM contracts. Now, scale for a three-hour recording session in Los Angeles is $90 for sidemen, and double, or $180 for leaders. He then informs the "musician" that he is to kick back the extra $90 to him. Nice, smooth and profitable. . . Ninety tax-free bucks for the "musical genius."

It is financially advantageous for producers to be members of the American Federation of Musicians. So, they get into the union at all costs on any pretext or ruse. Casual cocktail party bongo slappers become "Latin specialists." Beach party tambourine rattlers become "percussionists." And drunken spoon players are listed in the AFM directory under "drummers." AFM memberships allow producers to participate in recording benefits. Being bonafide "musicians" is a Fraternal affiliation that brings dollars. Producers add themselves to AFM session contracts as leaders and side men and collect $180 or $90 every three hours for doing little more than foot-tapping in the control room.

In certain cases, artists are unwittingly victimized by double-billing production practices. Artist contracts stipulate that all recording costs must be recouped from accrued artists' royalties before royalties can be paid. Therefore, double billing inflates recording outlays, which minimizes artists royalty returns. The artist is, in effect, paying for his producers' malpractices. Similarly, all inordinate or whimsical production expenditures have a diluting impact upon artists' royalties.

Artists who have contractually committed themselves to production companies, often find that they are slaves to a sad situation. The production company calls the shots on what the artist records, how he performs, and what is "best" for his image, his career, his life. These artists are industry eunuchs—castrated, helpless souls who have been absorbed into an antiseptic syringe to be blown up the ass of show business. And artists assigned to disinterested, surgical-staff producers are in no better shape. They, too, are a lost multitude wandering across the industry wastelands. Poor helpless bastards! And, more often than not, if success comes, it is the producer who wins the game and the pot. His rewards are sizeable. For instance:

The producer records an artist who is assigned to his production company. He sells the master to a manufacturer at a healthy profit. The manufacturer, in turn, promotes, merchandises, sells and distributes the record. The producer receives 10 percent of 90 percent of the suggested 98¢ list price for each disk sold, which will amount to a return of roughly, 8¢ per record. He pays the artist *tops*—5¢ per disk. He also owns the publishing on both sides of the record, which will assure him an additional income of 2¢ per record retailed, and at least 4¢ for each radio air play. In addition, the songwriter, who wrote the song that the artist recorded is under contract to his publishing company, production organization and personal management firm. Also, the artist is contracted for personal management on a 15 to 25 percent of gross deal. Not bad!

Some successful production companies have been fissioned into huge publishing, recording and management complexes with the power to woo the large manufacturers into "label deals."

Production organizations frequently create their own successful label identities. They build a label out of their artists' and writers' talent through specific handling and concentration of publicity, promotion and merchandising. Once the label is developed to a certain level of consumer popularity and industry acceptance, an acquirement is sought, and, boy, do acquirements come.

Remember, major manufacturers buy track records and the independent label boys play upon their gullibility. They ask for astronomical figures and impossible concessions, and they get them. They get them because all the corporate lawyers, and all the financial wizards and executive heads are fucked up. They really aren't in tune with the elusive nuances of talent and timing. They really don't have feelings and understanding for the street vibrations that gestate record consumerism. All they have are wide ties and hip lips, sideburns and funny suits with overwide lapels, Gucci shoes, and hideous fears of lost youth. So, they buy track records; clichés are for sale, and the industry impetuously buys; and the independents rub their hands and buy retirement homes in the South of France.

Often, record manufacturers involve themselves in label deals that are completely unrealistic and therefore damaging. Anxious to be associated with "winners," the manufacturers swallow up great chunks of undigestable fat that constipates their organizations. But all of the industry biggees want to be "hip." They want to be on board the image train and *choo choo* into the hearts of the youth market. So, they buy big, bad deals from shrewd, independent label bargainers.

Independent label guys appeal to the big industry types because they look good, talk about astrology, produce "groovy" rock artists and eat health foods, and of course they have good track records. The manufacturers shell out big peanuts with reckless abandon to these chattering, musical monkeys.

Here are some examples of major manufacturer stupidity:

Small Independent Label *A* sold his distribution rights to a major manufacturer. He received: (a) a $1,500,000 nonrecoupable advance; (b) a guarantee of 24 percent of wholesale price on every piece of his goods the manufacturer sold (24 percent of a 50¢ wholesale single record equals 12¢ per unit; 24 percent of a $2.30 wholesale album equals 55¢ per unit); (c) a $500,000 marketing commitment; (d) a provision for office space in the manufacturer's home office; (e) complete autonomy regarding advertising, cover art, liner copy, merchandising aids.

Super Small Independent Label *B* sold his distribution rights to a major manufacturer. He received: (a) a $200,000 nonrecoupable advance; (b) a guarantee of 24 percent of wholesale price on every piece of his goods sold by the manufacturer; (c) total autonomy regarding advertising, cover art, liner copy, merchandising aids; (d) a complete release relative to taped product.

New Independent Label *C* received over $800,000 cash on a loan basis. He also received maximum royalty percentages and full autonomy in the areas of merchandising, promotion, sales, art and advertising. By the way, the $800,000 has never been repaid as of this writing. It is rumored that the manufacturer is writing off the $800,000 as a loss.

New Independent Label *D* received $375,000 in front with partial recovery and a 24 percent royalty with no royalty reduction on tape, which wholesales at approximately $3.40 per unit. (Twenty-four percent of $3.40 will return the label 82¢ per unit sold.) The label was also guaranteed $150,000 per year promotional budget and the authority to place their executive promotional director in the manufacturer's national headquarters.

Another new independent label got a $225,000 nonrecoupable advance and a 20 percent royalty deal, plus marketing concessions.

Once label deals are firm, the formerly amiable producers and indie label heads become obnoxious pests. They drive the manufacturers mad. They suddenly become authorities on every aspect of manufacturing, engineering and marketing. They involve themselves in promotion and they bug national and field promotional people constantly with impossible demands. They hassle sales and handle merchandising. They become czars; miserable despots who behave childishly.

The independent labels often appoint special manufacturer liaison people. These label representatives are full-time vermin who constantly bother departmental executives, staff people and field personnel. They are whimpering little tattle tales who stir up trouble and create conflicts. They are either haunting the manufacturer's home offices personally or pestering people by telephone. Constantly, they demand and shout. They are usually obscene, overweight, career underachievers who piss away corporate efficiency. They tie up the time of workers who could, if they were not plagued by such inelegant cro-magnons, benefit their organizations. Departments are blitzkrieged daily with questions and bombarded with demands, criticisms, complaints and advice from these representatives.

Here's some typical examples of how these representatives "come on" to the various departments:

Sales: "How much did it sell yesterday? Is that all? Why can't you sell more? Do you have enough stock? That's not enough . . . make more. How many will you sell today, tomorrow, next week, next month? What! Why don't you know? Don't you know anything? Why is your Detroit salesman dragging his ass? I want him fired at once. What's wrong with San Francisco? Those bastards have only sold a thousand pieces. I want that entire crew fired. Why haven't we got stock in Des Moines? The group was in a record shop there, and the buyer never even heard of the album. Who the hell covers the Des Moines market for you guys? Who? Well, I want that sonofabitch fired. How the hell can we get trade listings without stock in the stores? What the hell are you running here, anyway? I'm fed up. I can't get any cooperation from you people. I'm going to see your president about getting your ass fired."

Promotion: "I just saw the new chart listings and how the hell can we only be at 110 in *Billboard?* Why the hell can't you guys get store reports? Your trade contacts are piss poor. I want better listings and I don't care what the hell you have to do to get them. Just get them. If you don't, I'll pick up the phone and call your superior and he'll get you off your ass. Why hasn't WPQ in Stinky Falls played our record? Who's your promotion man there? Get him on the phone and tell that sonofabitch I want play. I don't care how he gets it. Tell him to pay the jocks off, or get 'em laid, but get that goddamn record on that station. I don't need this crap. You guys don't know how to lay on hype. I'm a record man and if I have to turn queer to get play, I'll do it. I want air play and numbers, and if I don't get some goddamn results, I'm going straight to the top."

Merchandising: "What kind of crap do you call this? Look at this cover. Look at those borders. You call this layout? Look at this art. Who shot this? I want his name. I want that blind bastard fired. You call yourself an art director? You people don't know graphics. I'll have the goddamn work done by our artist, for crissake."

Artist relations: "I want a national tour lined up for Harry today. I don't give a damn how busy you are. I want it typed up and delivered to my office by this afternoon. Cost? Don't hit me with costs. I'm not paying for a goddamn thing. You people should be damn glad to have an artist like Harry.

Now, I want you to arrange hotels, interviews, limos in every city and be sure your promotion guys show up to help. What's that guy's name in Philly? Who? Yeah, that's him. Well, I want him fired because the last time Harry was in there, he refused to take him to the airport on Sunday morning. What? I don't give a shit where he lives. By the way, here's some bills for last night's press party at my house. Too high? Your ass. Look, you just read our contract, smart boy! Just wait 'til I talk to your president."

Individual producers also become industry czars. One particular case stands out boldly in my mind:

Back in 1966 when I was managing The Misfits, there was a small-time talent who headed a regionally popular rock group. His group had been together for some time and he was struggling to maintain a musical existence. His organization was a typical local, rock attraction. It was overly loud and raucous and groaned out weak, original offerings plus a healthy supply of "Wooly Bullies," "Hang On Sloopies" and "In the Midnight Hours."

After a discouraging fallow period, the leader finally decided to disband his group and pursue his musical career as a solo vocalist, which resulted finally in his securing a contract with a major recording company. His releases caused a slight stir in a few areas, but generally, acceptance to his recordings was slight.

While he was under contract to the label, he stumbled across a savage rock group. Impressed by the group's ability to generate crowd excitement, he negotiated a management-producer contract with them. Then, he produced an album with the group which he sold to his recording company. The album was a hit. Successive packages were enormously successful, also.

The producer, whose primary talent lay in his publicity abilities, milked every newsworthy possibility to expose his group. His management and business sense were true and his acumen was yielding bountiful returns. His stature was growing parallel to the group's, and so was his self-esteem.

Today, his group is a gold mine and he is its million-dollar babysitter. He calls the shots and they listen, and so does the record company that distributes the group's records and albums. They listen, listen quietly and listen good. They'd better, because this guy represents millions in billing, and record companies will poison their grannies for billing.

All demands are fearfully granted to this czar of rock. No questions are asked. Nothing is challenged by his manufacturer for fear of ruffling his peacock plumage.

Once, I am told, there was some dispute with him over royalties. Accountants were withholding payments for what, apparently, was a legitimate reason. Outraged, the producer refused to deliver to the label the tapes of a new album he just completed with his "super stars." Since the artist's albums represented hundreds of thousands in billing to the label, the label immediately caved in and paid out the questionable royalties. Another carelessly foolish industry act committed out of fear.

Self-ascribed production czars are born daily as illegitimate *enfants terribles* to an industry that sires them. Every successful recording artist becomes a "production genius" and the industry opens their budgets to them for costly experimentations. Like corporation idiots, the companies gamble millions on rag-tailed talent. One hit record, a best-selling song, opens the sesames of recordom. Even tenuous connections can lead to production agreements, and managers often establish themselves as production aces due to their successful artist associations. Everybody's in the act.

Top management gullibility, naiveté and impetuousness has pulled the plug from the industry's profit barrel. Ludicrously negotiated label deals, imprudent producer agreements, general production dishonesty, and double dealing and taking their toll.

In a recent press release, the president of a major record label that is declaring an approximate $8,000,000 fiscal loss revealed:

"The loss in the fourth quarter was accentuated by the need to make extraordinary provisions for artist and production contracts that are now considered unprofitable."

Well, *boys,* all I can comment is this:

If the musical meat packers continue to rule and management continues to play house on Ego Street, the industry had better prepare itself. Yes, brace itself for many turns at the fiscal whipping post.

8
Top-40 Radio— The Rock of Ages

Once upon a time, there lived an animal called traditional broadcaster. He owned the airways and walked ruthlessly with primitive self-awareness. The traditional broadcaster was king of the land, master of the programming jungle; a mighty force who presided over his domain unchallenged. But the absence of challenge creates a dangerous vacuum called complacency. And complacency breeds weakness and decay. So it happened with the traditional broadcaster.

The traditional broadcaster opened the doors of decay by sitting on his butt with his earphones over his eyes. His weakness bred new forms of broadcasting; little tadpoles that would grow into fat, nonsense-croaking frogs.

Back in 1953 when I entered the record business, the

traditional programmer was the dominant factor in the broadcast industry. The traditional broadcaster was the radio station that usually had three factors that assured market acceptance and domination; network affiliation, local newspaper ownership and a full-time operator's license with good power and frequency. Any station with such backing and potential was a power factor, and its influence upon the people it "served" was enormous.

This type of radio station maintained a sort of lofty, dignified position in the community. Its announcers read station breaks with booming projection. The news staff editorialized with pontifical resonance and the disc jockeys were smooth and professional, and segued from one "platter" to the next with dulcet composure.

The really important disc jockeys in my market were employed by Big Interest Radio, a prestige station of the first order. It had the paper, the power and network affiliation. I remember conducting my promotional visits with great respect for this hallowed institution. My presentations were always low-keyed with as much dignity as a small-time record sharper could conjure from his bag of musical legerdemain.

The station was located in an office building in a large eastern city. The broadcast facilities were on the 14th floor. Even the lobby entrance projected the typical big broadcaster image. The floors were inlaid tile of hexagon pattern. The walls were sparkling sheets of alabaster, rising twelve or fifteen feet to an ornate gilded ceiling. The elevator doors were bronzed in multiple sunburst pattern, and in the pattern crevices, one could spot thick cakes of dried polish, missed by some strong-armed custodial type. The doors gleamed like Montezuma's treasure, and radiant glints overwhelmed this miserable little record rat. The interior of the elevator was equally impressive. Walls were lined with highly-buffed mahogany panels over red velvet carpeting. Hand rails and floor selector escutcheon were also polished brass. A regular casket on cables that swept you upward to the silver microphones in the sky.

The main reception area was done in respectable decor. Deep green pile carpets swallowed your shoes. The walls were mottled with provincial oils and various awards that attested to the station's "public service concern." The furniture was muted, dark leathery and handsome. Even the john was a monument to effluviem. The walls, ceiling and floor were white marble and made the act of eliminating seem unholy— kind of like pissing into a crypt. The dignified austerity of the lavoratory always gave rise to the suspicion that a beef-eater was sitting in the next stall.

The management guys at this station were dignified-devious. You know, devious comes in all kinds of wrappers, but devious is still devious. In this instance, the "big boys" were Brooks Brothers corrupt. This is because the station manager was Brooks Brothers corrupt. Now, whatever the manager did, whatever business philosophy he espoused, and however he dressed, had direct mandatory impact upon the other stratas of management.

Occasionally, when emerging, hat in hand from the marble outhouse, I would encounter Dick Devious, station manager. He was always in some state of gray—wearing a blue buttoned-down shirt, red tie with small knot, black moccasin loafers with black lisle hose (the kind the hairs stick through). He would shake my hand firmly but nervously, and greet me with double-Martini breath. "Hi, kid. How's tricks?"

Staggered by his ivy alcoholism and agonized by the graven image of *1950* pressed into my hand by his class ring, I would respond, "Okay."

Snappy dialogue.

He would then scuffle on down the hall, murmuring executive inanities.

Undaunted by these amenities, I would proceed toward the fulfillment of my mission—that being to properly promote my records to the key disc jockey at this programming shrine.

The key personality at this station was Stu Black. He had a solid listener contingency and the retail effects of his programming were tangible. Stu's office decor followed the station continuity. It was quiet, dignified and leathery. He had a full-time secretary. She, too, was quiet, dignified and leathery. She would receive the visitors and preaudition all of the recorded product. Stu, himself, was a nice guy. He was quiet, unassuming and professional. His voice was obviously trained and even in conversation, it resounded authoritatively. He had musical background and could evaluate performances with knowledgeable perspective.

Jockeys like Stu programmed their own shows. They would arrive at the station several hours before air time and select the music they would program that day. The selections consisted essentially of material released by Columbia, Capitol, RCA and Mercury Records. There wasn't yet the surfeit of products created by multi-label releasing and most new artist's releases received at least some exposure.

The Stu Black type disc jockey was the ruler of Record America in the early 50s. And musical broadcasting was dominated by these "personality" jocks—jocks that picked their own music. The shows themselves were usually slow-paced musical segments broken up by the jockey's intermit-tant banal bullshit. No particular musical format was pursued. The air personality was the backbone of the shows.

Big power—big money stations were the undisputed kings of radio broadcasting. They had the prestige, the audience and those golden ratings.

The other side of the broadcasting picture was represented by the independent broadcaster. These indies were privately owned operations that did not have the advantage of net-work or newspaper affiliations. Indies were often handi-capped by weak signals and poor frequencies and were often "daytimers," (sunup to sundown) or were plagued with power reductions at nighttime.

In early 50s, most independent operations were func-tioning as broadcasting scabs in the major markets. They were mavericks, chipping away at their traditional rivals. They did reasonably well and occasionally held second-place ratings due to their aggressiveness, sensationalism and pro-motion, but the traditional radio giants were the biggees. They had the power, the papers, the politics, and they moved like whales through the rating waters, with the indies like little fish clinging to their backs.

In 1953, the most active independent station in the city was located in an old, second-story, walk-up accommodation on the south side of town. The station was virtually devoid of class, but did have a magnetic relaxing quality.

I'd call on the station at least twice a week because access was easy and air play on my product was marvelous.

The entrance to the place was an old gray side door at street level. Next door, was a seedy drug operation with a lunch counter where I'd buy coffee to spring on the disc jockeys. The counter area gleamed with eternal cheapness and the odor expelled from the lunch counter exhaust fan is still embedded in my sensory apparatus.

The steps that ascended to the station facilities heralded the madness that lay above. They rose, tongues of red linoleum, upwards through a sand-colored tunnel that was illuminated by an exposed 60-watt bulb. The flight seemed endless; the longest single ascension since *the* Ascension. A trip up those stairs with a bundle of 78 RPM records, two cups of coffee and six blintzes was no mean feat.

The stairs erupted directly into a catchall reception area. Desks, chairs, cabinets were all makes, varieties and vintages. Papers were usually strewn all over the cracked, imitation leather furniture. On the wall next to a water cooler was a cheesecake calendar depicting a shapely brunette leading an uncontrollable scotty dog whose leash was wound around her dress, exposing black nylons and garters. The calendar picture was subtitled "Oops!" The floor was covered with red linoleum. In fact, offices, rest rooms and control rooms were wall-to-wall with the stuff.

The men's john at the station was hardly a monument to anything. The walls were green plaster in shocking relief to the red floor. There was one urinal and one stall. The stall door had no latch, so I used to hold it shut by wedging a record into it (I knew they had some legitimate use!). In the corner of the room was a well-stained washbasin. A safety razor with rusty blade lived in the soap dish. Then, there was an eternal plastic cup, half full of stale coffee which repulsed my gentle senses. A cigarette butt was usually swimming around the murky mess like a soggy white whale. Quite a contrast to the marble pillars of Big Broadcaster's Temple of Apollo.

My contacts with the station manager and executive personnel was always informal and relaxed. Doors were open and entrances and exits casual.

Jack Miller, the key disc jockey at this station, was the antithesis of Stu Brown. He was loud and brash on and off microphone. His life was an ode to obscenity. His ranting and raving was legend, and record representatives fell before his tirades like corporate cannon fodder. I've seen him eject record people, both verbally and physically.

"Take that stacka shit and get your ass outa the station," was a typical Millerism.

Forgetting to bring him coffee was a heinous act. I never entered his control room without two giant sugar-saturated cups of the stuff. But for all of his brashness, there was a lovable quality about Jack. He was corrupt and admitted it; obscene and never hid it. I fell in his favor and we were friends during my long sentence in the market. We had brutal arguments and some days I loathed him, but through it all, the thick and thin of it, we remained allies.

Jack was a tremendous drinker, a couple of Martinis and three or four beers were everyday luncheon fare for him. I've seen him consume a quart of scotch in an evening. His appetite for food was equally ravenous. He ate like his food was his enemy, and he never paid—disc jockeys *never* pay.

Jack and his station were more or less typical of the independent radio operation in 1953; struggling, arrogant, little ranting animals waiting to rip the guts out of the big broadcasters and their time was coming—a strange phenomenom was in ferment that was to alter radio forever. A revolution was boiling in the stew pot of change that would end traditional broadcasting domination and sweep the myopic record industry beyond the reach of its own salvation.

Radio music during this period consisted of selections from the major manufacturers, Columbia, RCA, Capitol and Mercury. The music programmed had a great sameness. The jockey babble was free and easy and commercials were "dropped in" without attention to pace. All in all, early 50s radio was sort of media mashed potatoes and the traditional broadcasters and the major record companies were content to perpetuate the continuity of success. They were content, apathetic and unaware—unaware of a youth market that was growing restless in hot pants with money in its pockets. The soft ballads, lilting instrumentals and novelty recordings weren't fulfilling the subconscious needs of Teen America, an affluent generation in heat.

Inaudible to the general ear, strange sounds were rumbling; small record labels were beginning to make noise with a thing called "Race Music." Race Music was written and performed by black artists and it had great emotional honesty. Race Music was underground, and its exposure was relegated to a few blues stations in specific markets or to a special "race segment" during the independent broadcaster's programming day. In my market this segment was slotted at a weak rating period when the station was operating on low power. Originally, the Race segment was a filler—a throwaway, used to placate black communities and to pick up plus radio sales.

Slowly, but positively, the white youth market began focusing its attention upon rhythm and blues stations and black programming segments. Requests for race records began spreading beyond the black record retail retinue. Department stores, syndicate operations and neighborhood shops were being beset by requests for records by unknown artists on nondescript labels and the demand grew and grew.

Independent broadcasters began to awake to the explosive

potentials of this new music. More and more independent label product found its way to the turntables and the purity of black broadcasting was diluted by general acceptance and availability of the product.

The independent broadcasters realized the potentials and began to expose more indie product with hard-hitting intensity. A ton of energized cacophony split the airways and the youth market lapped it up. The disc jockeys screamed and played more music more often. The rhythm, the sound and the fury of energized roots-music captured the youth dollars and catapulted even the smallest station's ratings. Advertisers turned from the traditional broadcast stations to invest their dollars with the new contemporary media giant—rock radio.

And the growth continued. The old-line broadcaster had taken refuge behind tradition, and from behind dusty history books, stood fast in the wake of this "temporary" hysteria. The indies loved it and they captured the ratings and sent the traditionalists into retrograde from where they have never recovered their lost rating stature. More and more, the rock audience was assimilated into general demographics (people statistics), and the emergence of Elvis Presley was affirmation that the record and radio revolutionists had won the day.

Out of this victory, disc jockeys like Jack Miller became moguls. Their power was absolute. Their freedom unquestioned. They enjoyed a maximum of programming freedom. They exposed what they chose as frequently as it pleased them to do so. Their ratings were tops and no one hassles a winner.

The sudden surge of single record releases, created by programming acceptance of unknown artists, stirred heavy competition between record companies, publishers, artists and distributors. Dramatic, effective air play on product was now attainable by consistent pressure and hype on the Jack Millers of Rock Radio Land. Realizing the need for constant promotional pressures, the manufacturers created a new post, "Record Promotion Man." In the past, promotion had been handled by the territory salesmen as an adjunct to their sales duties. Now, however, promotion was the key in the pressurized atmosphere of rock radio. So full-time "hype artists" were hired to concentrate exclusively upon obtaining radio air play.

An avalanche of promotion descended on the rock disc jockeys. Air play was the trophy at any cost and the manufacturers sent their promotional pimps to buy up the plays. The promotional teams laid out the cash; dollars, women, clothing, meals, vacations. The gratuities given by the combination of promotion men, publishers, manufacturers and artists was staggering. The disc jockeys were pocketing tax-free fortunes while prostituting themselves and selling out their listeners with bargain-basement music.

This was a shawdowed period for the record and broadcast industries, and the greed continued. Then, the avarice backfired. The payola scandals rattled the cages of the music zoo.

Of course, the most distasteful aspect of payola is the fact that the listener is recipient of material which is bought air play. Quality is secondary to the bribe. The listener is not considered. Payola also thwarts the growth of creativity by limiting broad exposure of new artist and writer talents. The public was being cheated and artistic expression crippled by the gluttoned-fingered gangsters of broadcasting and record manufacturing. Now, for poetic irony:

The intervention of the Federal Communications Commission into payola practices scared the hell out of the broadcasters. They were scared shitless that they might lose their valuable licenses. So, these hypocritical prostitutes of public air moved immediately to prevent future incidents. In the past, the disc jockeys had had a free hand in selecting the music for their individual segments. They had been, essentially, traditional broadcasters in the sense that they had programming latitude and that they relied upon personality projection. Now, all of that would come to a panic stop.

Rock radio removed music programming from the control of the individual disc jockeys and established central programming in the form of a Program Director. Now, one person would screen all recorded product and determine what would be aired. The rock D.J. became an impotent automaton; Top-40 Radio was born.

Record companies, greedy little devils all, were responsible for the creation of a monster that would stifle exposure and assure the slow demise of single records as a viable sales entity. The classic story—"the musical Frankenstein who built the creature that would destroy its maker."

Rock radio pioneers realized early on that a certain rotation of recordings fragmented with commercials and proper spacing of time-news-and-temperature spritzes, generated audiences. The screaming Rock-Jock, plus hard-hitting excitable spots, got ratings. The rock format was crude, however; but now with the advent of central programming, a more rigid system could be implemented. So, Top-40 Radio evolved—a plan—a design—a formula, was poured into the electronic test tubes. The formula was essentially as follows: (a) limit the total number of musical selections; (b) create demand for new recorded product by consistent radio programming; (c) after demand is listener instilled, restrict audio availability by programming the selections on a daily formulated rotation basis; (d) insert commercials, time, news, temperature and other announcements with planned rotation. The theory: The listener whose appetite has been whetted, will stay tuned because certain selections will be aired with consistency in the programming cycle . . . Pavlovian trickery.

With the advent of Top-40 Radio, music became the hub on which the broadcasters played programming roulette. No longer was music important for its own sake. It was reduced to a vehicle to sell advertising by generating ratings.

Over the years, this genre of radio has evolved from traditional to rock to Top 40. So, today, the record manufacturers are saddled with format radio, a garrulous, insensitive giant that is a jailer of taste and talent, a constricting serpent created and perpetuated by their own involvement.

The establishment of central programming resulted in a new manufacturer-radio relationship. Suddenly, all new music had to be cleared through a central source. The program manager, or director, was now responsible for the station's "sound." He controlled an on-air aspects; hiring and firing of disc jockey personnel, jingles, public service, contests, gimmicks, promotions and music were all under his autonomous control.

The record manufacturer and the distributor's promotional representatives continued to descend like funny flies upon stations, pleading for exposure of their product. The program managers, snowed by an enormous workload, found it nearly impossible to handle the contacts and to screen the flood of new releases. So, at most major outlets, a new post was born—Music Director. The music director became the front man—the puppet—the dupe for the program manager.

Most of the music directors were headquartered in cleared-out broom closets or other such facilities that paralleled the size of their minds. In some cases, they took up residence in the bowels of the music library, ensconsed behind olive-drab steel desks and surrounded by mountains of 45 and 33 1/3 rpm horse manure.

Stations scraped guys off the walls to fill the music director posts. Errand boys, janitors, bootblacks, itinerant perverts, mailroom clerks and gypsy midgets were recruited. And occasionally even high school students, played music director on a part-time, after-school basis.

And the music director was king. He screened the music and made recommendations as to what the station aired. His role was absolute—a real record monarch. Record guys kissed ass and groveled, and these two-bit record runts loved it. All the record company representatives fought for his favor. It was sadly hysterical to witness a confrontation between the company reps and the music director of an influential station. Executives and local level people became song and dance men, entertainers, winers and diners. They would condescend, shaking in their shit, fearful of offending these unsophisticated little mountains of ego, and the music directors' heads expanded in proportion to the smoke that was being blown up their asses. They became gods—musical know-it-alls—$75-per-week tyrants and sadists who reveled in humilating and intimidating an industry that would sacrifice its integrity for a crumb of air play.

Program managers and disc jockeys were also romanced in the same servile obsequious manner. Every route to the airwaves was chartered.

I remember the endless lunches and dinners I purchased for radio people. What cagey tricks they employed to weasel free liquor and food. And they still do.

They secretly invite their friends and associates to partake of your expense account's benevolence. You arrive at a restaurant or club of your greedy guest's choice and are escorted to your table. The moment you make contact with your seat, it happens. People begin to materialize out of the carpet; aunts, uncles, wives, hookers, girl friends, secretaries, managers, mothers and others, appear, "unexpectedly" like guests on the set of "This is Your Life."

The holdup technique is another day-to-day radio wrinkle. If your appointment is, say, 11:30 A.M. or 5:15 P.M., the music director will begin a filibuster that would send any self-respecting Southern senator back to the precincts. Obviously, he has no previous engagement and no intention of spending his own money on such an incidental as food. So, he stalls. Eventually it's lunch or dinner time and you're hooked. After all, no record type would dare risk jeopardizing air play.

Then, there's the $100 hamburger.

A one-time music director acquaintance of mine was the king of all big spenders. He was a master. On the surface, he had all the suave of Porky Pig. Underneath, however, was the most subtle mind ever to bamboozle the corporate dollar. His reputation was renowned throughout the record industry. No one could surpass his artistry in such matters.

One day, my corrupt acquaintance pulled the old beforeluncheon stall on me. He kept me busy waiting. I waited while he answered phones. I waited while he allowed himself to be interrupted by fellow employees. I waited while he visited other offices. He listened to each of my new releases, at least twice, both sides. He chit-chatted and gossiped and philosophized with the profundity of a wart hog. But, what could I do? What could any record plugger do? You sit and listen and suppress vomiting with conscious, painful effort.

Finally, after nearly an hour's stall, he glanced casually at his watch. As if awakened from a deep trance, he started:

"Hey, man. It's 12:30. You had lunch?"

His timing and acting were flawless.

"Let's run down to the corner for a hamburger. Nice little place. Nothing fancy, but decent sandwiches. Okay?"

I was hooked. He straightened a stack of records, raised himself to a full five feet and pulled on a garment straight off the set of "Star Trek." He was unusually talkative and friendly, which should have been a grim warning of things to come. But, what the hell—a hamburger.

We walked to the corner in the sticky Midwestern heat. My date kept jabbering record talk and gesturing wildly, exposing ever widening perspiration rings. I was temporarily diverted by his repulsiveness—a malady which often engulfs me when I am in the presence of people consumed with the seriousness of business.

Suddenly, I was jolted back to unreality by the sight of squab flambe and the odor of Grand Marnier I was in the City's finest restaurant. I'd been had. The shifty, little bastard!

We were whisked tableside by a toothy maitre d'. A suspicious looking "reserved" placard stood in a field of linen and silver. When we were seated, I made a serious mistake. I unwittingly touched my napkin, which apparently was a high sign to my guests' confederates. They popped up like inflatable life rafts.

Introductions were made and extra chairs summoned. The bacchanal began. Gourmet conversation flowed as melliflously as the wine, and the pigs dug in with all the propriety of drunks at a free lunch. Two hours later, belches heralded the end of a $130 luncheon.

Music directors, disc jockeys and record people are, for the most part, unsigned brothers to the fraternity of show business. The element of theatrics is at their core, and the tinsel that touches the greatest star, reflects down to the lowest level of broadcasting and record manufacturing. The disc jockey and the promotion man feel as kindred spirits in the entertainment world. Every person who operates on the periphery of the entertainment circle, feels somehow drawn to the center where lie the golden rewards. The industry supports and is guided by this Milky Way of egos due to its own insecurities and ignorances. To recognize and fertilize great creative talent is noble and wise. To be guided and influenced by clichés, stupidity.

Record companies live in constant fear that they may offend a format broadcaster. Great caution is exercised not to upset disc jockeys, program managers, music directors. Even receptionists and secretaries are treated with utmost respect and gentility. People in the sales and promotional departments are also placated with whimpering silliness. The stations know this. They know that a record company's existence depends upon product exposure. So, they take full advantage. They push and shove and scream and the manufacturers bend and shuffle like Stepinfetchits.

The complete irony of this situation is that the format stations play only thirty or so selections anyway, and these consist essentially of established artists' records. Chances of the station "doing anyone a favor" is remote. The only favors they do are for themselves. They're concerned with one thing only—ratings. All the horse shit about public service and mirroring public tastes is lip service for the community and the FCC. If format stations are holding up a mirror, it must be to the public's posterior. The FCC grants each station the privilege of borrowing public air for three years. Commercialization is permitted, providing it's couched in a format that best serves the public's interest. Well, believe me, their ain't no public interest. Sure, the stations will deny this and expose logs and air checks as contrary proof, but it's all tokenism, bullshit. How much does format radio do to enlighten you and your community? Think about it. Turn on your radio, tune in and listen. Is it uplifting? Are you gratified? Are you thrilled that you, your family and community are the recipients of what you are hearing? This kind of broadcasting is test tube radio. It's produced, canned hash. Every record, every newsbreak, every weather report, every time announcement, all disc jockey patter, even commercials, are planned and canned to create a level of programming, a "sound" to excite and captivate listeners by conditioning through repetition.

The most feared term in the broadcast vernacular is "tune out." People turning their dial, people thinking for themselves, people sorting and rejecting and resisting is feared above and beyond all else. Broadcasters live by ratings, so ratings are almighty. The rating race must be won.

Ratings are determined by polls taken by private polling services. Pollings are underwritten by the radio stations. These services call a small cross-section of community households relative to station listenership. From this sample or measurement, station popularity demographics are compiled and converted into ratings.

High ratings mean less advertiser resistance, which means the station has a greater opportunity of selling radio commercial time. This is the ultimate purpose of the operation— to sell. When a station's ratings reflect favorably, the results are printed out, showing the competitive market comparisons. A number 1 rating in all time slots to all types of audience is the ultimate. The formula: programming plus listeners plus ratings equals dollars.

Now, salesmanship is a fine thing. I'm not against it. What I am against is what it has become and the practices that are applied to generate dollars. Hypocrisies are rampant in the marketplace, and dishonesty has become an ally to the cause of business.

In the race for ratings, all is sacrificed. To be number 1 is the broadcaster's goal, and every device and method is tested to sell programming formulas. Special promotions are constant format ploys. "Hit sheets" or "lists" are distributed to local retail outlets for consumer consumption. These sheets typically list Top-40 hits and picks being currently programmed by the stations. (A "pick" is a new addition to a station's play list.) The lists are compiled by a combination of retail information, national position and feedback, programming tip sheets, trade input, promotion-man hype, personal taste and voodoo. If a program manager is particularly fond of a record, he will arbitrarily move it up in the standings. Station picks always make *some* chart strides. They *must.* After all, no self-respecting program manager will ever admit to selecting a "bad" record. These lists are promotional gimmicks used to secure listener loyalty among the sub and early teen population. They're worthless, little sheets of propaganda that are treated as sacred documents by the format broadcast and record industries—regular musical Magna Chartas.

Then, there's the disc jockey propaganda machine: the good guys, the nice guys, the Mr. Wonderfuls, the Swinging Six, the All-Americans, Marty Miracle, Billy Big Heart, Sam Superb, Marv Marvelous, Wally Wit, the Great Gilroy, Henry

Healer, the Boss' Disciples, Arty Allheart, Junior Jesus, Gary God, Lean Gene Green, Foxy Albert, Fred With-the-Well-Bred-Head, Norvis Nimble, Ed Downs With-the-Pounds-of-Sounds, the AXZ Swell Persons, Mike Freight Who-Wails-All-Night, Housewife Harry, Danny Dean and His Teen Machine, the Great Ones, Waxy Tom Nerf, Cat's Ass Almont, Dr. Dooright, the Fab Five, the Mighty Men. The stations create these names and personalities. It's part of their campaign to make their on-air people into wonderful, warm-hearted happy individuals who are pristine and pious. If one would judge a format disc jockey by his press, promotion and personality projection, I'm sure his imagination would conjure an image something like this: A blonde, blue-eyed six-footer wearing a beanie, dressed in a white letter sweater, wearing white flannel trousers; on his feet, white fuzzy sweatsocks and tennies. In his left arm, a golden cocker spaniel (genitals missing due to artful negative retouching). In his left hand, a crucifix is draped over a scout manual. He is sitting poised on an American Flyer bicycle with red, white and blue crepe paper laced through its wheel spokes; a white knight, aloof and untarnished.

The broadcasters project their personalities as golden men. In reality, they are powerless, overpaid pawns of the major broadcast mill. They are molded to fit the format, to blend into the station's "sound spectrum." Their minds and imaginations thoroughly subjugated to the conformity of Top-40 mechanization.

Unfortunately, many of the key jocks fall victim to their own promotional propaganda. They become innoculated by the show-biz needle which immunizes them against anything outside of their own egos. Their public prominence sits heavy on their shoulders and they wear the weight like a garland of olive leaves—golden Greeks, strutting in the arena of hippy-dom. And the record people keep feeding these egos. They grovel and grin and beg. Relationships between the record man, the program directors, music directors and disc jockeys are "very close," "very inside." The record people are constantly attempting to "get closer" to them for special air play consideration. Naturally, the key Top-40 people are aware of this, but they condone the relationship for personal gains and benefits. And the record people know that they know, but still the charade continues and a mutual association of gross insincerity is maintained.

Occasionally strong commitments and personal friendships evolve out of these business dealings, but such commitments are rare. There is very little loyalty. The transitory nature of the industry has created a generation of users. If a particular person can't "do you any good," he is shunned, forgotten.

Another format-radio promotional device is the station "Appreciation Day" or "Gratitude Night." Annually, some stations show "their appreciation" to their listeners by sponsoring all-day affairs. Amusement parks are taken over and concerts are given at minimal admission charges for the fans. The record companies are the backbone of these events. Program directors demand free talent that will lend credence and attract crowds to these functions. The biggest names are requested without regard to cost and inconvenience. I've been witness to program managers going into fits or threatening profanity over manufacturer's reluctance or refusal to supply their biggest name artists. This is unusual, however, because most record companies are petrified at the thought of offending the programming giants. So, top talent is supplied at great disadvantage to the artists, who are forced to perform under outrageous conditions behind disc jockey masters of ceremony who possess all the show stuff of trained worms.

Format operations also organize ball teams to promote their station and further their images. The station disc jockeys make up these clubs. Promotional representatives frequently augment these aggregations which compete against school faculties, church clubs and various other community organizations. Stations place great value upon these athletic contests, and every drop of juice is squeezed from these promotional proceedings. Thus, team appearances are announced with consistent hysteria. Final scores are revealed with the pomp and solemnity of airline crash bulletins. The promotional guys participate in these events to "get close" to the jocks and program managers, and membership on a key station's team is weighed heavily as a cornerstone to air play.

In several markets, the key format station disc jockey has his own weekly television program. This TV segment is a powerful audience builder, and the cross-promotional advantages are obvious. The shows are generally played on Saturday in order to capture as much teen audience as possible.

These programs are spin-offs and carry-overs of the original TV hops, such as Dick Clark hosted. I'm sure you've stumbled upon some of these video monstrosities while switching between ball games on Saturday afternoon. The formats are identical. A very mod host, with shaped hair, mumbles and gyrates through an hour of cuts and dissolves. His patter is usually hip and his delivery is perforated with healthy quantities of "far out," "heavy," "right on," "groovy," and other garble which instantly dates him as a contemporary oldie. Little girls with big tits squirm in monster shoes to the big beat. This ensemble is usually referred to as something like "the Big Sound Dancers." The audience is composed of more keen teeners. Guys in elastic pants and girls in braless tank tops slither and grind and pop their crotches with the ferocity that would humble the coarsest sideshow stripper. It's television's answer to stag films. Dance contests are held. Guests are interviewed. Artists appear and schools are saluted. The disc jockey master of ceremonies stumbles, shouting through the whole mess, while wearing a "real groovy" fringe vest or American flag shirt, his insensitivity being his only genuine characteristic. Music is the backbone of the show. "The Top Tunes," hits, picks, "ones to watch," "hit bounds," and "super oldies" are the bridges over this river of shit.

Guest artists appear only to plug their latest recordings. I've never spoken to any artist who honestly enjoyed these video abortions. They hate them. And they usually are not even paid for their appearances. Unknown artists appear initially with alacrity, but after a few appearances, even they accept these situations as one of the promotional evils. Production and direction of these programs is most often amateurish. Backdrops are constructed from leftover backstage oddities, and all the old set clichés, like ladders, tinfoil and dangling balloons, are utilized due to budgetary necessities. Staging and lighting are stark, and the cued squeals and screams are bad—just bad.

Pressure for TV hop talent is great. Producers, program managers and disc jockeys prod the record manufacturers mercilessly for acts. Major talent is their meat, and they make unreal demands for the top recording names to appear on these two-bit video programs. Any self-respecting artist cringes at the thought of participating in these TV travesties, but driven by the fear that the radio station will not program his latest release as a retaliatory measure, he usually relents to the pressure. Every promotion man does his damndest to procure his label's artists for these shows. He is the middleman—the negotiator—and he acquiesces like a mass of quivering tapioca to the demands of the broadcast biggees. He pleads with talent, arranges transportation, lodging, parties and prostitutes.

A great number of the contests, TV and radio, held by the format broadcasters are underwritten by the record companies. Contest winners are awarded single records and albums as prizes. Whole libraries are given away. Dozens and hundreds and thousands of albums are awarded to lucky listeners and entrants, and the programmer doesn't flinch as he asks for voluminous quantities of product for giveaways. He approaches you as if it's totally right and proper to request anything—from albums to your sister. Never, does he reveal imposition. It's taken for granted that all requests are granted by merely rubbing the manufacturing Genie.

I could stock three warehouses with the product I've seen authorized for promotion. Requests are endless; they keep coming and continue to be filled without question or suspicion. Typical examples of promotional "write-offs" are: "1,000 Singles for Record Hop," "500 singles for Contest Prizes," "2,000 singles for Swing into Spring Contest," "300 Albums by X Artist for Television Giveaway," "500 albums for Tommy Klop Show Promotion," "250 Albums for Singing Jingle Contest Winners," "20 Complete Irving Anguish Album Catalogs for Fab Five Mystery Disc Jockey Quiz." And on and on and on without end, requests are made and requests are granted and free product flows like the fountains of Rome.

There are several appalling aspects to the promotional product-giveaway practice. First, the question of use is raised.

Does the promotion product, in fact, go towards the fulfillment of legitimate promotional needs? Proof of use is seldom if ever requested by the manufacturer or volunteered by station recipients. Secondly, a false demand is created by imprudent promotional merchandise withdrawals. If inventory records don't differentiate between promotional usage and sales movement, a false trend is created by this unexplained shrinkage. For instance, the movement of 3,000 pieces of album product can trigger reorders to cover the inventory gap; wasteful promotional efforts can be accelerated resulting in redistribution and renewed concentration on the item; sales thrusts can be generated and merchandising campaigns mounted to meet the demands for this "ghost hit." The third and most unfortunate aspect of indiscriminate giveaways is that artists are not paid on goods promoted and lose sales and valuable royalties as a result of promotional benevolence.

Firm denials to broadcasters based upon intelligent, business determination are rare. The record people crumble with hat-in-hand servility and the freebie giveaway promotional policy continues to drain away needless hundreds and thousands of dollars. The manufacturer takes the crap and keeps spending. So, are the rules in a poker game where fear deals the cards.

9
The Twenty-five Market Numbers Game and the National Trades

The success of a single record is measured, unfortunately, by its evolutionary growth on the national trade charts. A life-and-death struggle that toys with the destiny of artists' successes. Everybody in the business is constantly lipping chart potentials, trade picks, chart positions and chart life. In fact, the entire industry rises and falls upon the waves of a silly little numbers game that is a mathematical illusion.

In the sanctified chambers of record biz top management, chart talk bounces over bearded chins, careens over wide ties and cascades onto P & L statements. Sales, merchandising, advertising and promotion discuss charts with gray seriousness and reverence. Receptionists, secretaries, mail boys and guards are a legion of chart worshipers. Maintenance men, janitors, and cleaning ladies work after hours to exchange the latest chart gossip.

The charts. Oh, those charts—those electrifying, deflating, frustrating charts. The overpowering omnipotence of digital manipulation that rules a kingdom of musical mice.

The charts, like most everything else in the record industry, is a lie, told so frequently that it becomes something everyone believes in. What an irony! So many factors of phony hype and manipulation go into chart motivation that it's virtually impossible to separate created hits from hits arising out of natural musical acceptance. Actually, there's no distinction. All hits must still be generated and manufactured to some degree. The process is something out of Brothers Grimm.

There are three influential trade publications. In order of importance, they are *Billboard, Cash Box* and *Record World.* These trades, which are published weekly, contain the status of the top 100 single records in the country. The listings indicate the current numerical position of each record, plus the previous week's standing. Items showing rapid chart growth are noted by red dots. These red dots are referred to by tradesters as "bullets" and "stars."

The chart game can be likened to Uncle Wiggly or, if you will, musical Parcheesi, the object being to get the record "home" or to the number 1 position without falling victim to the Giant Wibble Wobble.

Upon release of a new artist's single record, the company issues disc jockey (D.J.) copies to its local promotional representatives. These mod delivery boys drop the records off at the Top-40 stations in their respective cities. Now, most major market Top-40 radio stations program only 35 records on a consistent rotation basis, thirty and five "extras" or picks, or hit bounds. These extras represent new additions and are essentially established artists' "sure shots."

The industry pumps out approximately 130 new releases each week. It doesn't take a seer to discern a lopsided supply and acceptance ratio. Only 10 percent of the single records released ever reach the charts and 95 percent of the product that does hit the Top 100 is relegated to established artists' identities. Top-40 programming restrictiveness makes infinitesimal the chances of new artists' records of hitting the charts.

If, by some divine light, a local programmer decides to expose a new artist's record, a whole chain of super manipulation and hype is set into motion.

When the programmer informs the local promotion man that he is "going on" his record, the promotional ace passes on the news immediately to his local sales distribution group, as well as his national superiors. He is very explicit in taking full credit for the programming windfall and feigns contrived sincerity and enthusiasm with the élan of a seasoned Shakespearean actor. After all, it *is* show biz, and no man is more thoroughly satiated with stardust than the record promotion potentate.

Now, the musical "meat packers" go to work. The local sales organization orders voluminous quantities of the record to "cover" the market in anticipation of consumer demands created by jingle-jangle radio. The record is shipped to every dealer, every rack jobber and every one-stop. Stacks and racks of the record loom like black smokestacks on retail counters all over the city. The company is ready—prepared— armed; every salesman becomes a vertible wholesale minuteman prepared to die for absurdity.

When a "big push" (I'm fascinated by the military jargon applied to American business machinations) is on a record created by solid air play, or when there is a competitive version of the same song, the major marketing wheels turn in ever-widening circles of mass-market madness. The sales department practically gives the record away. Deals are cut: buy ten, get one free; buy ten, get five free; buy one, get one free; buy none, get one free. Under-the-table dealing—back-alley bargaining.

In the case of a competitive version, the orders are "search and destroy." The competitive version is removed from stores, racks and one-stops. It's hidden, stolen or bought off with special deals. If the situation is really hot, other artists' best-selling records and albums are given as inducements to "lay out" the single.

Quickly, back to the charts.

The trades determine the profile of their charts by calling certain accounts in twenty-odd markets across the country. They call weekly on prescribed days. They also glean air play lists submitted by participating Top-40 radio stations. The air play sales ratios are weighted from this feedback and a determination is made regarding the relative chart potentials, positions, etc. . . . . Now, if both sales and air play factors are in strong correlation, a record will receive positive chart response.

The record companies make the trades aware of their new air play additions in the markets polled. So directed, the trades add the titles of the records to their check sheets for weekly solicitation.

The major trades are all currently located in New York City and each manufacturer contacts them personally, weekly, to alert them to air play and sales and to hassle them over chart positions and reviews. This is called "trade bugging" and is a big factor in the chart game.

While at Capitol, I appointed a full-time trade liaison. All the guy did, all day long, all week long, was to whine, dine and wine the trades. He was instructed to get favorable listings at all costs. I offered him handsome incentives to achieve prescribed chart assignments. Five hundred dollars for maintaining a "star" or "bullet," for moving selections into the Top 20, or for obtaining a local "breakout" was not uncommon. In fact, my trade liaison, could have become the highest salaried employee in the company, and ironically, the company would have loved it, because the charts, the numbers, no matter how false, spell success in an industry dooming its own existence by just such hypocracies and self-deceptions.

Quickly, back to the marketplace. With the record now being aired and mounds of stock swelling local retail bins, the sales and promotional boys begin to motivate propaganda. The trade and radio reporting accounts are "asked" to report positive consumer reaction to the record. The accounts are induced to falsify their reporting through generous donations of extra goods and free merchandise. Frequently, the clerks are bribed with cash to indicate "smash" acceptance to the selection. These gratuities are recouped via the expense-account route.

The combination of market loading and false reporting creates an illusion of hit potentials. The radio outlets move the selection higher on their lists and the national trades also feel the impact of the devious marketing artistry. If the record continues to reflect a strong sales life in the market, the trades will report this regional strength. This information gives impetus to other programmers in other areas to play the selection, and if they determine to expose the record also, the whole cycle of loading and reporting is activated again in those locations.

Three types of records arise out of saturation merchandising and false reporting: hit records, hit failures and "stiffs" (records that just don't make it). The hit record is one that has musical credibility. It would be a hit in spite of industry incest. The consumer would be honestly moved to demand retail stocking.

The hit failure is the record that really doesn't have it, but is born a bastard from the matrix of loading, phony bullshit and air play. The record enjoys a cycle of success, but not actual explosive life. It will often achieve high chart positions and it will get solid radio air play, but does it make money? Doubtful. When accounts are snowed with merchandise that receives spotty sales, they end up with a residue of stock, stock which is returnable to the supplier for full credit at printed cost prices. If the account receives free goods, back it goes for credit and the manufacturer loses money. The handling and crediting procedures involved in returns is crippling and engages clerical, sales and warehouse personnel in minus profit activities. The acceptance to the artist's next recorded effort is minimized at both radio and sales levels and his future is stilted. All in all, a negative success. I have known cases where money has been lost on "hits" due to overloading. The returns and return process obliterated the profits. It happens every day.

Finally, the "stiff." This record was doomed in the recording studio, and a tremendous amount of effort would have been avoided, had the tape been erased after the session. But some guy with "golden ears," some dismal little star-maker, salesman, programmer, promotion man, or busboy, some salamander of sound, sparked an Aurora Borealis of no-profit nonsense.

Returns on recorded product are gigantic, and the scrapping, a full-time job. I sometimes feel the industry creates mistakes to avoid boredom between occasional windfall successes.

Other methods of hype are instituted to perpetuate air play and sales and to influence trade awareness. When radio station phone lines are open to public requests, the artists, promotional people, and salesmen deluge the stations with calls. Also, the written request to the stations and to individual disc jockeys is a common "promo" ploy. How many times I've seen grown men writing backhand to simulate a teenage girl's scrawl, sending off banal notes like this to the disc jockey:

"Dear Groovy, Big Bill Gotthots. My favorite solid, groovy tune is 'Eat Your Heart Out' by the Vampires. Please play it, O Fab One, between 10 and midnight, from Edna to Delbert. Love, Little Terri Tighttits."

Sad, I know, but true. The promotional ballot stuffing prevails, and I've seen many a callous raised in the chart game.

Recently, a friend of mine who manages a promising new recording talent learned that his client's record was going to be "battled" on a key radio station in a small Midwestern city. Although, the station was located in a market of secondary nature, it had credence due to its relationship to the trades and other industry programming publications. Anyway, the station was going to battle the record.

Battling consists of pitting a group of new record releases— one against the other. Each record to be battled is played during a given disc jockey's segment, usually in the evening. After all the contesting discs are programmed, the D.J. asks his listeners to vote for their favorite from the group. The telephone lines are then opened and hot and heavy balloting ensues for a specific period of time. The record receiving the most votes, receives the dubious honor of being added to the station's regular play list for consistent exposure throughout the station's broadcast day. Therefore, the battle winner is national grist for the sales-promotion manipulation mill.

Eyes glazed with hit grandeur, my friend, his wife and the artist planed into the small Midwestern city and took a room in a local hotel. They insisted upon adjoining accommodations with three phones. Once situated, they turned on the local station and settled down to await the battle royal. Can you imagine? Three grown people, huddling over telephones with fingers poised. Los Angeles freaks staked out in a seedy hotel like the Dillinger gang holding out against the coppers.

After a time, the battle rules were announced and a special "battle line" number was given. When the word was given to vote, the freaky trio worked in a frenzy to dial for their record as many times as possible. When the voting was stopped, the group slumped to the floor, deflated bags of California hypo. Finally, the winner was announced. Their record lost.

The national trade publications announce the next week's chart positions for singles and albums every Wednesday. This affords the manufacturer the privilege of knowing the chart status of his product before the publications hit the stands on Monday. Chart time every Wednesday is the most traumatic interlude in the industry's work week. Everything hangs upon the chart positions.

The results of seven days of scuffling, screaming, lying, loading, cheating and begging will be judged at chart time. Favorable charts will absolve the most gross and despicable criminal. Poor charts condemn the honorable, the upright, the virtuous and true. The charts are an amorphous, consuming thing, a product of dishonesty and a revelation of information that is ambiguous beyond explanation, but the charts rule. Men are fired and hired, careers are exchanged, arranged and obliterated. One week, a record executive with good charts is a saint. Next week, with poor charts, he's a boil on the corporate asshole.

I have witnessed the termination of good promotion people due to temporary chart weaknesses. When the charts reflect negative, all is forgotten and loyalties and friendships dissolve. No one questions business conditions. No one points fingers at poor product. There's no analysis of potential sales distribution or credit problems. When the charts are gloomy, no one looks for clouds. Realities are overshadowed by emotional insecurities.

The unrealistic effervescence over favorable chart listings and numbers is just as destructive, or more so, than the down-side aspects. Good chartings blind the business biggees to all underlying problem areas: excessive returns, credit hangups, poor management, stagnant advertising, stupid promotion and weak product are alike buried under the fertile soil of a flourishing chart garden.

Frequently, when a manufacturer is basking in the fluke success that touches all eventually on the musical merry-go-round, he is impervious to the lessons of the past. He forgets the dry period and why they were foul, and the advancing drums of doom are muffled by the din of passing profits.

When a label is hot; when they are experiencing great sales success due to public acceptance of one, or maybe two, of their artists, they tend to become paralyzed by the situation. Other artists are ignored. Catalogs are neglected, and building below the threshold of their success ceases. Temporarily, all is rosy. They're hot, and greed, ego and shortsightedness prevail. But the charts, like all of show business, is a fickle female—capricious and inconsistent. The heydays end and the success moves on to play benefactor to others, who, too, become ensnared by the sirens of the charts. Like Ulysses, a wise record executive should demand to be lashed to his swivel chair while passing through favorable chart waters.

Other inducements are also attempted in the chart game— manufacturers pressure for picks and listings relative to advertising expenditures. Positive reviews alert record buyers and radio programmers to the "best" new releases. Good picks are given to artists with consistent hit histories and new artists' offerings that favorably strike the subjective attitudes of the reviewers.

Manufacturers are also constantly applying ad pressures. When charts don't shine favorably, or when reviews don't meet expectations, the crap hits the conveyor belt, and the company executives explode at the trades. Promotional directors exercise their endless repertoire of obscenities and even presidents erupt. The trades are threatened, chart methodology is questioned and advertising schedules are pulled. And man, do the trades hate ad cancellations.

I suppose there's some law of corporate kenetics that spawns the evolution of trade publications. Farmers have their journals, ad executives have *Advertising Age,* and even little old seeds have their catalog. All trade magazines, periodicals and publications arise out of some inner delight their readers get from keeping on top of professional gossip. I was always intrigued by my machinist uncle's grave look as he thumbed through the contents of *Nuts and Bolts Monthly.* The irony of a trade is, of course, that it exists by virtue of the industry it reflects. How, then, can it ever wax unfavorable about itself? The music trades are typical. They're always topical, hard-hitting and positive. Musical funny books chock full of jargon and junk, perpetuating antiquity. I've never, ever, read a poor live-performance review in the trades. They're all glowing, and obviously placating to advertisers. All groups are grand—singers sensational and bands big, and the way they're written is actually laughable.

I remember when I was a district sales manager, back in Cincinnati. Every Monday evening after dinner, my wife and I would read the record revues aloud. We would swap revues. She would read a revue from one trade and I from another. God, it was hilarious. Even my children, who were then sub-teens, would rail with laughter at these garrulous proceedings.

Let me give you a typical record revue and then an explanation:

Adrian Slurp—Languish Idaho (2:56)
   (Prod. by Lefty Luck and Millard Fluke)
   (Glutton, BMI—Lynch Finch)
Slurp returning from a golden outing on "Lipstick on My Navel" steamrollers this Finch evergreen into another Top-10 Teener. A jock's delight, and op's will harvest many spins.
   B/W
"Twenty Pounds of Tongue" (3:35)
(Larceny, ASCAP—Poop Edwards)

Here's the review decoded: Adrian Slurp is the artist, and he has recorded a song entitled "Languish Idaho," which is two minutes, fifty-six seconds in duration. The producers are

Lefty Luck and Millard Fluke. The song is published by Glutton Publishers, which is affiliated with BMI. The writer is Lynch Finch.

Slurp's last record was a million seller entitled "Lipstick on My Navel." His performance on "Languish Idaho," which is a standard tune written by Lynch Finch, is outstanding and is predicted to be a Top-10 recording due to teenage acceptance. The programmers will love it and the juke box operators will receive numerous plays. The song is backed with "Twenty Pounds of Tongue," which is three minutes, thirty-five seconds long, and is published by Larceny Publishers, an ASCAP affiliate. Poop Edwards is the writer.

Then, there are special features, like an editorial on the state of the industry, articles on the quality of product, the futures of recording, the responsibilities of the industry to the common man, the effect of photographic resolution upon field mice in Baton Rouge, how video cassettes will make pornography family fun in the 70s, and other probing, poorly written snatches of pompous garbage.

Then, there's a column announcing personnel changes— hirings, firings, transfers and promotions. Usually, the same names and faces reappear on a kind of prescribed rotation basis. A guy who was fired last month from X company, has been fired from Y company and rehired by X company to replace a guy who quit to take his job at Y company, etc., etc., etc. People tumble around the employment hopper like popcorn, a pitiful legion of itinerant freaks. Ah . . . what glorious madness! And that's the trades! That's the national charts, the mass of numerical jabberwocky that rules an industry of juvenile giants.

10
℘Publishers—
the Musical White
Slavers

What grotesque memories I have of those musical meat men, those little greedy-fingered midgets in the shiny suits, sitting behind Swedish Modern façades. I sometimes feel these guys are born bald, overdressed and bent over holding cigars. They're a breed unto themselves; carry-overs from the musical ice age into the insanity of entertainment present.

There are many young people in publishing, also. They're regaled in the latest garb of hippydom, peeking from behind scruffy hair with cool eyes. They look right, talk softly and hasten to tell you that their "heads are together" and that their aim is on the creative target of free, artistic expression. But, underneath the Mickey Mouse T-Shirts and behind the patches on old Levi's lies lurking little bald, overdressed, bent over, greedy-fingered midgets with cigar stained Masonic rings.

Now, music publishers exist from the revenue obtained from their copyrights. Copyrights are documents on file in Washington, D.C., that protect a particular work from piracy and invasion and secure positive ownership, authorship, etc. These copyrights are secured on a government document identified as "Form E." The publisher, or owner of a song, submits copies of his work, along with $6 to the Registrar of Copyrights in Washington. The copyrights sleuths run the application through a relatively informal procedural process, and in about two weeks, one copy of the Form E is returned, sealed and certified with an assigned copyright number. The copyright is now the sole property of the applicant for 56 years.

The publishers subsist upon monies paid out to them for performances of their copyrights. So, the name of the game is to amass a substantial catalog of active copyrights. These catalogs are compiled by tying up the publishing rights to reams of unattached material. The old shotgun, or as my farmer daddy would say, "If you throw enough crap against the barn door, some is bound to stick," theory is practiced. So, most material is locked up to rot in file cabinet drawers. The chances of a publisher devoting any honest time and effort to an unknown writer's material, are remote. Allow me to pose a typical example:

Say you write a song that you feel is pretty good. You play it for a few people and they are also enthusiastic, and someone suggests that you should "do something with it." Unprofessional, and therefore, unaware, you contact a friend who has a friend in the entertainment industry. It's suggested that you contact Oceans of Greed, a big publisher with "all the hits." You call Oceans of Greed and relate that you have written a song that has gotten a strong reaction from many who have heard it, and you need professional advice and guidance.

Now, providing that the receptionist doesn't fluff you, she will give you the standard spiel:

"Well, Abe Wonderful screens all new material, but he's not available right now. He's in a meeting. In fact, he's been in a meeting for eight years and he's leaving for London tomorrow for six weeks. If you mail us a lead sheet and a tape of your material, I'm sure Mr. Wonderful will review it when he returns."

So, spirited by publisher receptionist spiel number 6, you hasten to do a home recording of your selection and have a lead sheet (words and music) notated by a local guitar teacher and with dots on paper and a melody in your heart, you mail your musical masterpiece to Oceans of Greed. Then, the big wait.

Six weeks, seven weeks, eight weeks—three months go by, and still no response from Mr. Wonderful or Oceans of Greed. Disturbed, you call the publisher, explaining that three months earlier you had submitted a song as instructed, but to date, no answer.

Publisher receptionist replies, "Well, Abe Wonderful screens all new material, but he's not available right now. He's in a meeting. In fact, he's been in a meeting for eight years, and he's leaving tomorrow for London for six weeks. If you mail us a lead sheet and a tape, I'm sure Mr. Wonderful will review it when he returns."

In desperation, you explain again that you have submitted the material, exactly as requested, but you've heard nothing. Apparently sensing your frustration and anger, the receptionist puts you on hold. Then in a burst:

"Abe Wonderful here. Yes . . . yes . . ."

You go through your hoops for Mr. Wonderful, who also apparently senses your anger and frustration.

"Just a moment. Let me see if I can locate your tape."

He puts you on hold. Now, at this moment, Abe and the receptionist are rooting through a giant Rinso carton full of tapes submitted by other would-be Bacharachs. All tapes that come in are usually tossed in a can, where they amass waiting to be returned with a form rejection letter.

Your anger and insistence have paid off, however, and your tape is going to be rescued from obscurity. Abe's back:

"Yea . . . I have your tape. It was right here on my desk under some papers. I'll listen and get back to you."

Next day, you receive a phone call from Oceans of Greed: "Abe Wonderful here. Say, I listened to your tape and it ain't bad. Tell you what. I'll shoot you over some songwriter's contracts. Sign 'em and mail 'em back and I'll see what we can do. Okay, baby?"

Next day, you receive the agreements. They are two feet long, printed in minute type face. You sign and return them. Oceans of Greed now has you by the balls for 56 years.

In capsule form, this is what has transpired: You wrote a song. You taped it at your own expense and paid out of your pocket for lead sheets. You mailed it to a publisher who had no intention of ever auditioning the material. You called and bugged them and they sensed you were pissed. So rather than have some irate clown running around the streets bad-rapping their firm, they consented to audition the tape. They liked it—not crazy about it, mind you—just liked it. But rather than risk another publisher absorbing the material into his catalog, they tied up the song with little or no intention of ever really working your material.

Usually, this is where it all ends—a songwriter's agreement in the file, dust for the eons.

Standard practice in the publishing domain is to tie up anything that "sounds good." Songwriter's agreements are as meaningful as the publisher's intentions, which are rarely more than nothing.

Daily, writers sign agreements that tie up their material. The emotion that is the result of creative labor is slipped mercilessly into a musical cesspool. Fledgling writers are flattered by publishing agreements and are vulnerable lambs in the musical slaughterhouse. The alarcity with which new writers sign over their works is appalling and sad.

A legitimate publisher is one who operates on a level of honest activity, one who screens all material, one who personally sees writers, one who catalyzes, motivates and nurtures writers with ability along a path of growth through positive direction, one who openly rejects the material which is not suitable along with constructive suggestions and criticisms; and most importantly, one who only signs songwriter's agreements for that material which he intends to actively work and promote.

Unfortunately, the publishing business is infested with paper people—tie-up artists and piece-of-the-action boys.

Let's dig into some of these practices and explore the negative results they effect:

The lifeline of recording success is material—a good song. One that is solid, both lyrically and musically, is usually the springboard to successful recording artist's careers. In fact, an artist can experience lifelong popularity due to his association with a strong piece of material. For example, Tony Bennett with "San Francisco," Jimmy Dean with "Big

John," Bobby Gentry with "Ode to Billie Joe." Proper interpretation of great material can be a meal ticket to entertainment longevity.

The development of a new artist identity requires strong material suited to his talent and stylization. Obviously, an artist must have some vestige of distinctiveness and talent, but this is meaningless without his coupling it with proper material. Initially, the artist and his producer search for a great song that will gain him industry success through radio programming and record sales. So, every brain is picked, every catalog is gleaned, every publisher is contacted in the search for "the song," in the quest for "the hit."

Now, if luck plays benefactor and the right musical collaboration is arranged, and if all the other subtle little manipulations pay off, the artist can get his "Top-10" treat. When this forced miracle occurs, naturally, he's an "overnight genius," the talk of the trades and the subject of *very* inside industry garble.

The artist and his producer are now spiraling, spinning, tumbling across a sky of success, rising like inflated balls of fat into record Nirvana. Once they begged, now they demand; and this is one of the ladders into the tomb of forgotten talents. They want a piece of everything. After all, they're "Super Stars," and they deserve it.

When a publisher brings them a new song, they demand half the publishing rights. When a talented writer shows good material, they demand the copyright. In other words, if they can't get a piece of the action, they won't record the song.

God, how many times I've heard major producers cry for split copyrights!

"Yea, Jim. I dig the song. Tell you what I'll do. You assign me half of the rights, and it'll be Randy's next record."

And how often I've heard big stars apply pressure upon groveling publishers and writers:

Suddenly, a piece of the song becomes secondary to the quality of the material, and the sound of money in the coffers becomes more poetic than the lyric, more glorious than the melody. The artist and producer are no longer recording the best music, they're recording the most lucrative copyright deal, and the career-destroying effects are disasterous. Broadcast acceptance is diluted, sales are minimized and the artist lapses into musical limbo and opens franchise restaurants or becomes a nightclub hack.

I can be understanding and sympathetic to the struggling writer who gives up a piece of his mind to a producer or artist for a potential hit and a catalyst for his career. The insecurities of the writing profession are enormous, and, therefore, it's easy to be intimidated by people in positions of strength and power. The creative struggling talent is a beggar. I can forgive his crumbling, but I'll never be able to excuse publishers who sell out their copyright, who give side deals and reduce rates. Publishers generally are musical vultures, but those who sell out are carnivores who eat what they regurgitate.

I don't believe the average person has any idea of what a tremendously lucrative business music publishing is. The return for the amount of effort and outlay is phenomenal. Let me give you some idea of what a hit copyright can return and how publishers and writers are remunerated:

Payments are made on mechanicals and performances. Mechanicals cover the sale of recorded parts, records, tapes, etc. Performances cover broadcasting, TV, live performances, movies, etc. Two major performance organizations, BMI and ASCAP, monitor performances and collect and distribute accrued performance monies to publishers and writers. For purposes of this example, I will quote BMI performance rates only.

Mechanicals resulting from phonograph record sales, are paid to the publisher by the record manufacturer at a rate of 2¢ per selection sold. This 2¢ is split equally between the publisher and writer. BMI pays the writer 2½¢ and the publisher 4¢ for each radio broadcast performance. Sales from piano music returns approximately 25¢ to the publisher and 5¢ to the writer for each copy sold.

With these basics as a foundation for computation, let's compute the royalty benefits and residual monies generated by a typical million-seller record. Here we go:

Now, one million single-record sales at 1¢ per copy (that's the publisher's share) equals $10,000. As a rule of thumb, the number of performances will approximate the single record unit sale, in this case, one million units. BMI performance rate for radio air play is 4¢ to the publisher, so 4¢ times 1,000,000 equals $40,000.

An album resulting from a million seller, should sell approximately 250,000 copies. This "follow up" album will contain the hit single, plus usually three or four other songs by the same publisher. Frequently, all songs in the album are published by one house. Let's assume the publisher in this instance has four selections in the album, including the hit. Now, four selections computed at a rate of 1¢ equals 4¢. Four cents times 250,000 equals $10,000.

The sale of piano copies, or sheet music, is another lucrative aspect. Let's estimate that the sheet music sales, as a result of a million seller, are 100,000 copies. Now 25¢ times 100,000 equals an additional $25,000.

Mechanicals	$ 20,000
Performances	40,000
Sheet Music Sales	25,000
TOTAL	$ 85,000

This is the approximate minimum revenue generated from just the hit single and this can be considered only the immediate royalty garnered during the life of the hit single. Keep in mind this covers only the initial mechanicals, performances and sheet music sales and does not take into consideration, other heavy royalty areas such as television, movies and other performances.

If the song is musically adaptable to many interpretations, it will become a standard (Example: The Beatles' "Yesterday"), and other performances called "coverages" will perpetuate royalty returns; the dollars, like the melody, will linger on and on.

Publishing is big business and every little cat with office space and a phone is getting into the act. They know the enormous financial potentials. They know there's a sea of credulous, guitar pickers, housewives and bellhops who may have a song. They're spinning their webs and waiting, with songwriter's contracts stuffed into the pockets of their iridescent suits and bluejeans. So, beware, young writers, don't hum too loudly and please sing softly in the shower, for who knows what stealthy little greedy-fingered midget may be lurking in the shadows. Check for cigar smoke.

Music publishing as originally structured was an honorable profession, industriously motivated to maximize the potentials of songwriting talent. It had some good people committed to honest purpose and imbued with some sensitivity and talent. Today, there are still a handful of good guys, but essentially, the business is overpopulated with self-centered skimmers, who merely run their hands over the top where the fast dollars lie.

11
Artists

There are two kinds of recording artists: talented megalomaniacs . . . and megalomaniacs.

That's right. Only two. Don't tell me about all of the subtle in-betweens and all the wide diverse personality types. Don't tell me I'm being unfair. Don't tell me I'm generalizing and making a sweeping statement, and all that other pseudo-humane, hippy-dippy nonsense, because I won't buy it. I know the artist types, and dearies, there are only two.

Talented megalomaniacs are the truly artistic, creative artists that contribute honest works that offer lasting entertainment. They're the super stars who open up their mind valves and pour forth vats of creative juice that you and I lap up with great satisfaction and delight. Their works make the profits that build and sustain the record industry. They're the guts, the down-inside people who *are* the record business.

Everything else is surface; oil floating on the fluids of their creativity.

Great artists, by their very nature, are possessed by demons. Down inside each of them resides a horny little devil that possesses their soul. This demoniac possession is necessary, absolutely necessary, because it is the thing that sets them apart. Some call it drive—some determination. I maintain it's demoniac possession. It's a devil that tells them they must be great, that they must succeed at all cost, that nothing else matters except fame.

All great artists are possessed; I'm convinced of it. I have known many, and in every case, I've discerned the demoniac motivation. Oh, sure, on the surface, they often appear mild and serene, quiet and reserved, regular "guys on the block," Little League organizers, scout leaders and big brothers. But, that's just the hide of it, their face to their public. Down in their bowels is that churning, spiny little pitchforked demon, prodding and motivating.

I've known "down home" imaged artists who are totally monstrous. On the surface, kindly padres. Underneath, a seething glob of tyrannical lava.

I recall once when I was working with one of these "Mr. Warmths." The artist and I had just checked into a hotel. We retired to our room and ordered some drinks. We waited. Nothing. After half an hour elapsed, I redialed room service and firmly requested immediate attention to our order. Another half-hour elapsed. By this time the artist was beginning to boil. His anger grew and grew. He couldn't conceive how any establishment could give "him" poor service. It was a dastardly affront, a slam to his ego. His anger grew into uncontrollable proportions. He called the desk, the assistant

manager, the manager. He screamed, ranted, raved; an un-
believable display of unrestrained paranoia. By the time the
boy showed with the order, "Mr. Wonderful" was a raging
fool. He grabbed the poor kid and began slapping him about
the room. I was flabbergasted. I intervened and finally sanity
was restored. The incident caused quite a stir, to say the
least, but a lengthy, diplomatic meeting with the management and a hush-up hundred to the shaken room service boy
subdued the matter.

Most artists never resort to such childishness. Generally,
they are cordial and gentlemanly, but still, however, they are
possessed and driven people, and thank God for us that they
are.

Possession acts with great attrition upon the creative artist,
and day-to-day role playing, flattery and success creates
unique, egocentric, frustrated individuals. But, they carry on.
They have to. They must. Because, they're victimized by
themselves, and the pressures are great.

One famous female artist, I recall, was always a nervous
wreck before performances. She would worry and stew over
lighting, audience, arrangements and accoustics to the point
of self-distraction. To allay her fears and tension, she would
take a tranquilizer, followed by a stiff gin chaser which
usually calmed her until show time. Once on the stage,
however, she appeared totally relaxed and self-confident.

A male vocalist that I knew, who was at the top of his
profession, was outwardly the most casual person alive. His
movements were controlled, his speech soft and unhurried.
He was so relaxed, so very, very cool, but inside, he was a
shambles. He would fret and worry and panic over every tiny
incident. His stomach was an ulcerated mess. It caused him

constant pain, but his suffering was never evident. At show time, he appeared calm, cool and relaxed. Another talent trapped by the demon of greatness.

Some great artists are extreme ego nuts. They primp and rearrange themselves constantly. Every car window, store front, all reflective surfaces become their vanity mirrors. One particular guy even carried a small compact and was forever checking himself out in cars, on the street, in elevators and in restaurants. Other artists must be the center of attention always, regardless of the situation. Some concentrate on drawing flattery out of others. They ask, "How do I look?" "What do you think of my new shoes?" "What do you think of my latest record?" "I've just lost twenty-five pounds. Can't you tell?" "Would you believe I have a daughter twenty-three?"

Then there are the sex freaks, the artists whose greatest talents are apparently between their legs. Sex, sex and more sex is their forte, and they spend every moment in the pursuit and fulfillment of their sexual desires. I traveled with one artist who was taken over by sex. He talked sex at breakfast, in clubs, in offices, at press conferences, at meetings, at luncheons, cocktail parties, radio stations, in alleys, on planes, in rest rooms, at dinner with anyone, everyone. He had stories and crumby little anecdotes about his conquests. Sizes, shapes, races and creeds were disclosed. Every little detail was meticulously described with grotesque gestures and dramatic grunts and groans. His joke repertoire was also an endless prosaic revelation of carnal carryings-on. He never stopped, and he propositioned all females regardless of physiognomy or age with the subtlety of a ranch hand. I swear to you, this guy would have raped the little match girl. Once he had me cruise the streets of downtown Cleveland so he could look for pick-ups, and when he finally induced a filthy, overweight soul into the back seat of my car, he consumed her as if she were a box of buttercreams.

There are various and sundry kinds of artistic nuts sprinkled over the top of the record industry sundae. There are stars who become authorities on all subjects and talk profound talk on talk shows about Viet Nam, politics, medicine, racial problems. Then there are the amateur psychiatrists and psychologists who dig deep into the chasms of unconsciousness with authoritative pomposity. And then, the ecology buffs, who should recycle their heads. And the astrological maniacs, spinning in intergalactic confusion. The diet nuts, and of course, the health food preachers, who should have a carrot shoved up their egos.

In contrast to the artists who are talented megalomaniacs, there are the artists who are just plain old megalomaniacs. This group of recording artists are possessed by demons, too; demons and no talent.

Unfortunately, the industry supports and, to a great degree, is guided by the untalented megalomaniacs, who are permanent, destructive fixtures, whose greatest creative achievement is their ability to waste corporate time and dollars. But, again, the industry buys "track records" and its impetuousness to do so has fostered the growth of these noncreative parasites. Artists with just one hit record are often recognized by the industry as "geniuses" and the industry pampers these individuals and sells out to them. Big deals are given and unrealistic autonomy is placed in the hands of these low-talent and high-egoed "miracle boys." And the geniuses suck up the company's money and generate great corporate conflicts and losses.

Artists and managers are closely aligned, and, therefore, we might profit in some managerial disclosures. I won't spend much time on these boys, though, because my low opinion of most managers won't allow me to afford them much attention.

Most managers are 15 percent rake-off boys, who ride the coattails of creative talent. They're usually the "hippest" of the "hip" in their talk, dress and actions and are always on the business scene to "protect the interest of their charges." (That's what *they* say. They're actually protecting their 15 percent.) Managers like to pick up unsuspecting talent and sink their talons into established acts for fun and profit. A manager with a going artist can make plenty of dough and is in a position to attract other talent and good record company deals. Successful managers, managers associated with hit talent, can always call nice shots with the record companies, because the companies wish to keep them happy. After all, they just might bring the record companies some "groovy" new act. So, the record companies pat them on their heads, pay them compliments and buy them lots of drinks and stuff.

Managers always claim that they are working on their artist's behalf. Their artists are their main concern, and their only reason for living is to protect their artist's interests. For shame, such nonsense. The 15 percent is the thing. The 15 percent and side deals from record companies, kickbacks from club dates and revenues from phony bills.

Managers are also passengers on the industry bandwagon. Hell, they drive it! They sit on top with 15 percent reins in their hands (7½ percent in each rein) whipping taste and trends with villanous glee. And they're record company buggers, too.

In their perpetual struggle to "protect their acts' interests," managers join the ranks of producers, production company people, independent label liaison, promoters and artists, who make careers out of being overbearing jerks. The managers bug sales, promotion, merchandising, art and artist relations departments constantly.

Yes, managers are phantoms who apparently hide in the record companies' attics so they can swoop down and protect their 15 percent whenever so motivated. They hang around record companies like ceilings. On any day, at any given time, a manager is in some record company, somewhere, asking questions, demanding, and working at being obnoxious. So, if you want to see a real live species of Managerius Percenta, just drop by any record manufacturer's offices and look through the bars of the corporate cage. They'll be there, and they're easy to spot. Just look for very pale-looking, horsey-toothed, gum chewers in clothes that say "trend."

12
He Was
a Beautiful
Person

In nearly every major city, there's a music-industry hang-out, a spot, an *in* place, a haunt where all the self-acclaimed record "heavies" congregate, swap stories and tell lies. Nearly every noon and evening, these record rendezvous are jammed with the cliché characters of the biz.

These establishments are usually ornate little bistros of beefsteak and bullshit that make fortunes overcharging the record biz clientele. And the clientele loves it. Why, they would be insulted not to pay inflated prices, for they are, after all, the flamboyant "leaders" of a business that does everything big: big hypo, big falsehoods, big expense-account padding, big overselling, big payola, big kickbacks. "When a bigger business is built, the big record business will build it." Tabs at these places run like grocery store tapes; $75, $100, $200, $300 dinners, are consumed by the devotees of affectation with regularity and passion.

Maître d's give award-winning performances, and their credulous guests bloat with pride and garlic. First-name identifications are snapped. Chairs are pulled. Menus are presented with poetic gestures. Cigarettes are lit and unpronouncable dishes are explained in Berlitz dialects. Every caste of record man is fitted with ego elevators. His armchair becomes his throne; his fork, his sceptre, and his pepper shaker, the Holy Grail. From the moment the record types enter these restaurants until they exit, every theatrical trick is used to flatter them out of their too-tight britches. Great outpourings of "affection" are often exchanged between the maître d's, waiters and their guests. . . . When particular heavyweights enter these establishments, loud salutations ensue; back-slapping, hand-shaking, poking, cheek-patting and hugging. The last time I witnessed one of these customer-proprietor embraces, it was revealing to witness the owner checking out table service over his "lover's" shoulder. Just like a whore eating an apple during intercourse. These restauranteurs understand record people and they pile on the syrup. It's good business.

On any given night, a visit to these industry watering holes will reveal the same crowd of "beautiful people." A few weeks ago, I visited one of these joints after a two-year hiatus, and the same characters were there, telling the same old stories. Nothing had changed. Time had been suspended as in a painting, and like a giant fresco, the whole scene of hypo and horse shit hung there, a classic statement on the reality of American business decadence.

While I was there, the "producer of the week" arrived. There is always a currently "hot" producer gracing the atmosphere to extoll his own "genius" and to blot up the phony congratulations and compliments. The producer was lavishly outfitted in an apparent attempt to imitate Captain Kidd. His white slacks were pushed into knee-high, rawhide boots. The boots were criss-cross lace-up jobs with top fringe that flopped conspicuously when he walked. His tan, buckskin belt was at least five inches wide, and fringy, and the guy's initials were burned into its side. His shirt was light blue with a gull winged collar and puffed sleeves. The first three buttons were open, exposing a barbed wire chest. He was back-slapping and getting slapped back. People were shaking his hand and congratulating him on his recent "hit" triumph.

"Man, your record is heavy, really heavy. It's beautiful."

"Yea, man, yea, man? Hey, thanks. Yea, it's doin' real well. Number 6 with a bullet in next week's Billboard."

"Wow! That's a heavy trip. Number 6. No kidding? That's great, man. You deserve it. I was just telling Herb here that of all the cats in town, you were the nicest. You're a beautiful person, man."

"Thanks. Thank you."

He passed around the room, shaking hands politically.

Over in the bar area was one of the major publisher's braves. I say "brave," because he was dressed as an Indian, beaded moccasins, Levis and a patchwork shirt. On his hands were all kinds of turquoise jewelry set in silver. His belt buckle was turquoise, too. Around his head was an Indian headband, grainy with beadwork designs. He was drinking firewater and speaking with forked tongue to a local promotional heavy about how he convinced a major artist to record one of his company's songs.

"I said, look, Jack. Hey, look, man. Let's face it. This song is a blockbuster! Rick Adams is really writing heavy stuff. The guy is really together. I told him like half a dozen other artists was holdin' the song and that he was really out-ov-it if he didn't record it. No one else was actually holdin' the thing, but, what the hell! What did he know? So, I said . . ."

The Indian rambled on to his glazed listener.

Several other producers were there, also, making their voices available to nearby eavesdroppers. Certain phrases and words were purposely lifted to penetrate the din of the crowd. "Hits," and "We wrapped up this TV deal," and "Well, Elvis told me last week," were noticeably projected to impress the surrounding juvenile gentry.

Several record people were there with stars. Showing up with stars is always a very impressive thing to do. It reflects upon the host favorably. It establishes him as a real heavy-weight. The stars were the real center of attention. People were hanging all over them and buttering them up with compliments regarding their "heavy" recordings. And the stars were eating it up and saying "heavy" a lot and thanking people for being so "beautiful."

"Heavy" is an ever-present industry term that means powerful, sensational, great. To be referred to as an industry heavyweight is to receive the highest compliment. It means you're great—a real winner. Heavyweights are born out of the elusive gold dust of dubious deeds. Record breaking (establishing a hit record) establishes industry heavies and reputations evolving out of record breaking are often lifetime success mantels, granted to and worn by the record breakers. And, the record-breaking heavyweights acclaim themselves "geniuses" for single-handedly "busting one loose." What magnificent self-deception. Record breaking is a complex process involving trade picks, friends, television, timing, trends, sales, hypo, broadcast acceptance, artists, advertising, merchandising, payoffs, falsifying and luck, luck, luck. When a record does occasionally make it, though, every little worm crawls out of the woodwork to pick up his credit for "breaking a big one." These types, these "heavyweights" are ever-present overindulgers at America's record restaurants. They're always there, jiving and reminiscing about their record-busting prowess. And, typically, the industry buys the stories and buys them drinks and tells them that they're beautiful people.

Guys who aren't "beautiful people" are lightweights, and people who don't associate with beautiful people are lightweights, and the promotion men who don't "bust hits" are lightweights, and the people who don't frequent the industry bistros are lightweights.

"Wow!" is another piece of industry jargon and has been picked up from the youth and musically hip. It's an expression used often by the record set.

"Beautiful" is a most *in* term that is used excessively by industry types. I define "beautiful" as Las Vegas hip because the expression welled up out of the caverns of show business, not from the streets. "Beautiful," "beautiful person," "beautiful baby," "sweetheart," "sweet sonofabitch," "wonderful human being," "gorgeous" are all Vegas hipisms adopted by the recording robots. Here's a Vegas hip conversation:

"Look, baby, Sid Fink is a sweet sonofabitch; one of the sweetest people in the business. Your money's no good around Sid. He's a sweetheart."

"Yea, a beautiful guy."

Or: "Hey, Jim. Let's go over to Sam and Eddie's for dinner. They got gorgeous food."

"Yea, okay. They serve a beautiful steak. Meetcha there at 7."

"Beautiful."

Other industry jargon is picked up from the youth and the

musically "hip." "Right on," "hip," "rip off," "turn on," "together," "where your head's at," "get it together," "power to the people," "overcome," "wow," "far out," "trip," "laid back," "dude," "really," "get it on," and "heavy," are expressions that are used by jazz musicians and on the streets among those of the youth-rock culture. Industry people pick up this terminology in order to identify with and to be vicariously associated with what's "going down" with the kids. In this way, they feel "hip" and "with it" and part of the scene. They feel then, knowledgeable about music, dope, and the youths' tastes and feelings, and they use this "awareness" to get through to the kids by selling their culture back to them. Fools, idiots. Just another one of the practices that has crippled the record industry. This and all the overproducing, overreleasing, overpromoting and overadvertising of "the kids' music" has finally backed up in the marketing drains and has created an overflowing cesspool of stagnant sound. The kids are wise and fed up, and no longer buy the crap dumped on the market by the pseudo-hip industry gristle-vendors.

I recall, as I was leaving the industry oasis that evening, wending my way to the door through the gauntlet of insincerity, being stopped by a couple of promotion men who were sitting at the bar. They'd been discussing, they said, Adolf Hitler, and they were wondering, even though he had been a sadistic demagogue, if he also had warm and compassionate characteristics. They solicited my opinion.

I thought for a moment. "Adolf Hitler? Yes," I replied, "he was a beautiful person."

13
The Kickback Kids

Once when I was a little guy, running my electric train through my papier-mâché mountains, my father approached me. He asked, "Roger, what do you want to be when you grow up?"

Without hesitation, I replied, "Either a brain surgeon, president of General Motors or a movie star."

"No, son. Forget all that. Take my advice and become a purchasing agent."

Purchasing agent? I thought. Gee, dear old dad must be nuts. What could be more lofty, more financially rewarding than my choices?

Little did I realize what sage advice dear old father had given me. To this day, I reproach myself for not heeding his heady advice. But, after all, that's behind me. Hindsight. That was before my eyes were opened by the American Kickback College of Hard Knocks.

In the record industry, purchasing positions are just one area for lucrative kickbacks that are perpetrated against the corporate interests. There are many other ways and means of skinning the corporate cat, too. Let me uncover a few:

Advertising agencies historically charge 15 percent for their services. This 15 percent is either added to advertiser's bills, or deducted from the agency bills as an allowance for legitimate agency involvement. In any case, the ad agency makes 15 percent. Now, people who control industry advertising dollars can angle for a piece of the action. Here's how:

The corporate employee in charge of company advertising will work out a kickback arrangement with an advertising agency. He'll often ask for and receive one-half of the agency commission, or 7½ percent. A million dollar budget is often available, and the employee's kickback on this kind of expenditure would be a tax-free $75,000. Pretty good.

Sometimes the industry employee will anonymously open his own outside agency. He'll appoint a front man to maintain it, handle paper, billing, production, etc. He then runs all of his company's advertising through his own business. His only operating expenses are rent, for usually a shabby, one-room office, a front man's minimal salary, phones and supplies. He will also, in these cases, charge back all "production costs" to his company, which are over and above his 15 percent commission take. Production costs (layout, copywriting, announcer's fees, studio costs) are often double-billed.

The people who deal with suppliers and service organizations, are also in a juicy position to cut side deals for nice tax-free benefits. Fifty-fifty deals are cut with outside artists, for instance. Either the artist will be asked to submit double bills or fake bills for work that's never been done. After bills are paid by the company, the artist will kick back one-half cash—no questions asked.

Paper suppliers and printers are also hit for kickback splits. Deals are worked out for inflated billing, or again, billing for nonexistent work.

Sales and merchandising aids purchasing (divider cards, counter displays, mobiles, album jackets, streamers, presentation books, sales kits, floor browser units, wall hangers) is another open road to kickback holidays. Again, deals are worked out with the suppliers for balloon billings and/or fake billings.

Outside services and suppliers are almost always willing to engage in the kickback carryings-on and why not? It means substantial, consistent business and swell personal pocket money. Also, accounts payable seldom, if ever, questions the bills. They have no justification to question a statement containing the signature approval of an authorized departmental employee or head. So, they just pay and the kickback kids play.

Deals are also set with independent promotional guys. National promotional people work out "steady employment arrangements" with them for special "considerations." Independent people are retained. They bill the companies, the bills are approved and paid, and the independent boys return a check for one-half of their "wages" to the national promotional wheeler-dealers. Nice tax-free flowers blooming in the mailboxes of industry heavies.

Bonus kickbacks are good, too. National sales and promotional offices often work out sweet deals with field personnel. While on field trips, the national heavyweights arrange special bonuses with those people "they can trust." After arrangements are agreed upon, national thieves issue phony bonus checks to their field confederates, who in turn, cash them and kick back one-half to their bosses. Preapproved expense-account padding is also practiced for no-tax fun and profit.

Shifty credit managers rake off tons of booty through artful credit deals and internal manipulation. Say an account owes a record manufacturer $100,000 in past-due billing. Well, the credit salamander hops a plane, under the pretext of straightening out the problem, to visit the payment violator. Once behind closed doors on a one-to-one basis, the credit creep makes his pitch. He offers the account a "special" deal. If the account will give him $20,000 cash, he will guarantee that the $100,000 arrears deficit will disappear from his company's credit records forever. Faced with an attractive settlement alternative of 20¢ on the dollar the account will usually spit up the twenty grand. The credit manager then does his "pencil work" and the case is closed and everybody's happy. The credit man is $20,000 richer, the account is thrilled by the 20¢ deal, and the sales department is elated that the account is again "open" to buy.

This reminds me of a particular case history: There was this credit manager who worked for a major New York-based label. He was a most creative charlatan who, with the aid of his girl friend, worked out a clever way of swindling his company. His girl friend was a departmental head for the same company. Her job was to scrutinize and approve all advertising claims submitted under the company's co-op advertising plan. A strategic position that could be used to their mutual advantage. Aware of this, the credit manager established fictitious accounts for the company record. The account addresses were the apartments and homes of tight-lipped friends. The couple then worked up phony advertising bills for the façade accounts which the girl would approve and forward to the accounts payable, who would issue checks without question. The company was drained of thousands until finally, the couple was tripped up due to a sales-account analysis.

Contracts people play their little games as well. Say a well-known artist's contract is nearing option time and the contract man wishes to pick up some casual spending money. He will contact the artist and propose a deal. He'll tell him that he will work with him to negotiate a tremendously lucrative deal if the artist will kick back a few thousand for his intervention. If the artist agrees, and he usually will, the contracts administrator will enthusiastically recommend to his company that the artist be resigned on *his* terms. Naturally, companies never want to lose valuable talent and this, coupled with the contract negotiator's endorsement, will usually assure the artist of a lopsided, lucrative deal.

Or, let's assume that an artist has a multi-million dollar offer from a competitive label, and therefore wishes to terminate his current label association. In this case, he will, on occasion, approach his contract negotiator and offer him a sizeable chunk of money for being negative relative to resigning him. If the negotiator agrees he will inform his company that he feels the artist is "over the hill" and will recommend an option drop.

Warehouse inventory theft has always been an industry problem which has cost companies and artists millions. One company had a ring operating out of one of its major-market wholesale distribution centers. Clerks, salesmen, warehousemen, shipping clerks, credit people, promotion men, sales managers, trucking lines and accounts were banded together in a monumental and history-making heist that shook the industry. Day after day, thousands of albums were blatantly stolen from inventories by the combine. Finally, a plucky little accountant's suspicions were aroused, and with facts and a natural talent for uncovering shady situations, he set about building a case against the suspected thieves. With the aid of plainclothesmen, he scrupulously compiled incriminating information that was sufficient to break up the ring.

Voluminous quantities of merchandise are withdrawn from stock under the guise of "promotional goods." This merchandise is "written off" on official documents that "explain" the inventory usages and assure proper inventory control. Tens of thousands of records and albums are pulled from warehouse inventories every month to meet "promotional demands." The sad fact is, however, that a great portion of this merchandise is never utilized for the prescribed promotional purposes. It's sold for cash or traded for goods and services.

If a sales manager, salesman or promotion man wishes to pick up extra money, he will complete one of the inventory withdrawal forms. He will indicate, for instance, that a certain radio station needs 500 albums (usually a hit) to cover a recent promotional contest. He'll deliver the promotional withdrawal form to the warehouse, where the 500 albums are pulled from stock and then loaded into his automobile. He will then deliver the albums to his fence who will generally pay him 50 percent of the wholesale price. Or, the merchandise will be worked off through a radio station. In this case, the albums will be mailed directly to an accomplice at a radio station, who will in turn sell the merchandise and split with the manufacturer's representative. This method is safer than the preceding because it removes suspicion by establishing proof of delivery.

Promotional write-offs are also made for goods and services. Stores that handle other products in addition to phonograph records are particularly desirable fences because they afford unlimited exchange possibilities. Suits, appliances, jewelry, furniture, sporting goods, motorcycles, houseware, camping equipment—you name it—are exchanged for records and albums. Exchanges are usually made wholesale against retail. Example: ten $2.50 wholesale albums for one $25 retail blender.

Under-the-counter buys are infinitely more desirable to fences than the regular distributor purchases due to the improved wholesale to retail ratios, and, the fence can exchange or return this merchandise to the distributor for full cost credit. A regular $2.50 wholesale album, picked up under the counter for $1, will net the fence $1.25 come return time. Many fences buy under the table just for return advantages. These "deals" also allow fences to retail product at tremendous consumer savings. So, if you have ever wondered how some retail record outlets can offer such attractive bargains, this is one of the answers.

Excessive promotional stock withdrawals have forced most manufacturers to instigate means of self-protection. Today, most companies mark all merchandise that is going to be used for promotional purposes. Holes are drilled, perforations are made, stickers are applied and special "promo" labels are affixed to promo products.

Marking has only curtailed slightly the promiscuous promotional practices. Labeling has, though, reduced the return problem somewhat, but the stickering and drilling has done little to minimize dishonest dealings. Stickers can always be steamed off and a warehouse confederate will always "forget" to drill promotional goods for a piece of the action.

I knew one guy who paid off his home loan with money he received from under-the-counter selling of promo albums. He had a fence who, due to his trans-shipping connections, could use all available hot merchandise. So, he wrote off tons of albums weekly to supply the demand. He'd load his VW trunk, passenger seat, back seat, floor—a regular record runner, this character. And when he was fully loaded with his musical white lightning, the wheels on his bug would be splayed out under the weight of his cargo. It's been estimated that he pocketed over $20,000 in less than 12 months.

An acquaintance of mine purchased a new Corvette with money received from the sale of stickered promotional albums. He discovered that steam, properly applied, would allow the stickers to be skinned from the albums, leaving the jackets unscathed. Very ingenious. An assembly line was activated in his kitchen. He, his wife and son systematically peeled stickers in a real sweatshop operation. Steam billowed. Crispy curtains wilted. Stickers flew. His Corvette was red.

A whole lot of drilled, perforated, stickered and labeled merchandise is sold too. Rates are lower, though, due to the fact that the marked items can't be as handily returned and don't have the consumer appeal of clean product. Fences will pay 50¢ to 75¢ per album and 5¢ to 10¢ per single record for marked items. Unknown and unpopular artists' selections bring less.

Promotional merchandise, also, is often swapped for flesh. Yes, that's right—flesh. Girls are frequently bought with "good stuff," and, therefore, I'm certain that many hookers have excellent record collections.

People in the record industry are always swapping promotional records and albums for something or other due to the massive availability of promotional goods. Everybody's selling, swapping, stealing, bargaining, trading and robbing. Someone should pass out blackjacks and masks. This is promotional overkill that doesn't kill anyone but the company. "Too much, too often" seems to be the industry code, particularly when it comes to promotional goods. Stuff is ground out and shipped to employees in quantities that generate shipping costs that would save Biafra. Bulk quantities of promotional goods are indiscriminately issued and subsequently misused or sold by field representatives. Review copies are sent to reviewers who don't review, and reviewers also sell review copies. All key industry personnel receive new singles and album releases by costly direct mailings to their homes, and the duplication is incredible. Sometimes the same selections are mailed two and three times to the same people, who, of course, sell, swap and trade. Top company executives weasel into neighborhood record stores with stacks of new releases to sell and trade. High level bargaining by low level people.

Product theft and subsequent under-the-counter dealings costs the manufacturers millions in lost sales, unearned credits, ambiguous inventory data and retail price undulation. As a result, artists, publishers, producers and writers lose royalty fortunes.

Then, there's the multi-million dollar drain created by double billing, phony statements, falsified advertising claims and affidavits, side deals, forged bills, credit ploys and contract double dealing. Is there any end? Yes, for the manufacturers!

14
Grammys
and Country Music
Awards

The National Academy of Recording Arts and Sciences and The Country Music Association awards are given for outstanding artistic music industry achievements. The NARAS and CMA presentations are made yearly at lavish, formal affairs and are attended by industry hierachy. Everyone who's anyone is in attendance at these proceedings. Record industry executives, publishing heads, musicians, songwriters and recording artists turn out all tuxed-up for the occasion. It's an important night. It's prestige time and people arrive in gusts of contrived enthusiasm and exchange greetings with the usual show-business flare for transitory sincerity.

NARAS and CMA award winners are determined by a procedure of nominating and balloting that proves the time-honored adage: "There's strength in numbers." Allow me to acquaint you with some of the details:

Associate (nonvoting) memberships in NARAS are $15.00 per year. Active (voting) membership dues for NARAS affiliation are $20 per year. To be an eligible, voting member, you must qualify in at least one of the following categories:

As a vocalist or singer who has recorded at least six commercially released selections (a selection is equal to one side of a single record; and individual album cut is considered one selection; six album cuts or sides equal, therefore, six selections).

As a leader or conductor who has received label credit on at least six recorded and commercially released selections.

As an A & R man or producer who has personally produced at least six recorded and commercially released selections.

As a songwriter or composer who has received label credit on at least six recorded and commercially released selections, or who has written or composed a work which has been recorded and commercially released by at least six different recording companies who have given you label credit.

As an engineer, that is mixer or other type of engineer, who has lent a direct artistic contribution to a final recording. Proof of your participation in at least six recorded and commercially released selections is mandatory.

As an instrumentalist or musician who has participated in the recording of at least six commercially released selections.

As an engineer with no less than six recorded and commercially released selections to your credit.

As an art director, photographer, artist or designer who's been credited for cover design in connection with at least six recorded and commercially released albums, or as an annotator or literary editor, who's been credited for liner notes in connection with at least six recorded and commercially released albums.

Or as an individual who has participated as a spoken word talent (comedy, documentary, drama, etc.) on at least six recorded and commercially released selections for which either label credit has been given, or for which you can prove satisfactory participation.

If you aren't eligible for any of these categories, you can qualify for an associate membership if you're actively identified with the recording industry.

If you qualify, just whisk off your money and proof of qualification to NARAS, Sunset-Cahuenga Building, 6430 Sunset Boulevard, Suite 503, Hollywood, California 90028. Soon, you'll be instated as a member in good standing.

If there's a decided twang in your musical tastes, you might like to become an active, voting member in the Country Music Association awards as well. There's nothing to it. Joining's as easy as rolling off a pile of grits. Simply submit $15 for yearly membership, or $150 for a lifetime (perish the thought) affiliation to CMA, 700 16th Avenue, South Nashville, Tennessee 37203. You must, however, qualify under one of the following categories as:

An advertising agency affiliate, who is working with any recognized advertising agency.

An artist who earns his living through public performances and recording activities, or a musician who plays a musical instrument, sings, dances or gives dramatic or comedy dialogues.

A booker, promoter, agent, ballroom operator or artist manager.

A composer, who has either BMI, ASCAP, SESAC or a

legitimate publisher affiliation and at least one song recorded and commercially released by a recognized label.

A disc jockey currently employed by a licensed broadcast organization as an on-the-air personality.

A music industry trade paper affiliate with at least one year's experience in the field.

A publisher with either a BMI, ASCAP or SESAC affiliation.

A professionally employed executive in the radio or television industry.

A record company employee, working for a recognized, financially responsible record manufacturer.

A record merchandiser, who's actively engaged in the wholesaleing and merchandising of phonograph records and tape.

A nonaffiliate who is active either directly or indirectly in the field of country music, either presently or in the past.

Yearly, NARAS mails prenomination eligibility lists to its voting members. CMA mails a similar sheet to *all* of its members. These lists represent a first ballot, and nominations are solicited for specific categories of artistic performance, and the members are requested to write in their choices covering each category (male vocalists, female vocalists, motion picture soundtracks, bands, arrangers, instrumentalists, etc., etc.). The members make their categorical nominations and return the first ballots. The ballots are then analyzed by an unbiased accounting firm, which audits them on a plurality basis, and the nominees receiving the greatest pluralities, in their individual categories, are determined to be finalists. These finalists' names are then printed on a second and final ballot that is distributed to the voting contingent, who in turn, check their choices and return the ballots for conclusive tabulations.

Obviously, award winners are selected on the basis of a majority vote. It's pure and simple. The old democratic way.

Simple, true, but unfortunately, not very pure—because the industry does everything in its power to overload the voting. Within many major manufacturing organizations NARAS and CMA memberships are mandatory. Promotion men, salesmen, artists, engineers, executives are required to enroll as members and their dues are either paid directly by the company or they are allowable expense-account deductions. Every effort is made to beef up the subscription and get out the vote. In some instances, the companies distribute specimen prenomination lists and final ballots along with direct orders from the top to vote as indicated.

Major manufacturers plainly have a tremendous weight advantage. They employ hundreds who can be regimented to attack the ballot boxes and, as a result, the big manufacturers usually sweep the awards.

Allow me to give a typical example of how, say, a publisher can stack the NARAS and CMA awards in his favor:

First, he enrolls every member of his staff who can qualify for the NARAS and CMA memberships: writers, composers, arrangers, engineers, field representatives, production people, and even administrative and clerical personnel. He signs them up, pays for their memberships and then dictates exactly how they nominate and vote. He demands that they nominate and vote for his writers, composers, producers and arrangers. Further, he cajoles and campaigns outside his organization for write-ins and votes. If possible, he will try to establish himself as head of a local NARAS or CMA chapter, a good political position that can carry weight and place him in a position to influence other voters to cast in his favor.

There are some industry people who tackle NARAS and CMA overloading with frenzied determination. They work like madmen soliciting nominations and votes from other members, and their campaigns take on the fervor of good old red, white and blue politicking. *Boom, boom* goes the drum for ballot padding. *Crash,* go the cymbals for industry prestige.

So, the majority rule applies and determines the winners in the music industry's horse race, where goofballs of phony pluralities often dope the real winners. And, therefore, questions are raised: Did the truly great creative talent win, or are the winners losers? Who won what, really?

15
Hookers, Hats and Horns

My flight arrived late in Miami and I deplaned into a beautiful, balmy Florida night. Boy, what a relief from the hot and sticky Midwestern summer. I walked through the exit ramp and headed for the baggage area.

"Hey, Rog."

Christ, it was Harry Markham, the Atlanta manager.

"Hey, Rog. Grab your stuff and meet me up in the lounge. Some of the guys up there. Already got broads and everything."

Nice greeting, I thought, from old Harry, family man and parttime religious fanatic.

I ripped my bags off the conveyor and rode the escalator to the terminal main floor. I spotted the lounge at the end of the area. Big, blue neon sign bent to simulate longhand. LOUNGE, it quivered.

No way, I thought, and headed for the exit.

"Hey, Rog!"

It was Harry again, waving and gesturing. I was trapped. He ran over to me, all red-faced and panting, his body pungent with that indelible bar smell of smoke and alcohol.

"Come on, man. Here, give me that bag. Come on. Lotta guys already here. Kellerman, James, Blanchfield, from the Dallas operation and Hugh Smith, our Cincy rep. We got in couple of hours ago. Been drinking ever since. That Kellerman . . . That sonofabitch . . . Is he funny . . . Sonofabitch is really funny."

Kellerman always impressed me as a sonofabitch, all right, but never funny.

Inside the lounge, the boys were tearing it up. They had literally taken the place over. Blanchfield and James were arm wrestling, while one of the two "girls" they had picked up shouted encouragement. Smith was sitting with his arm draped around the other girl watching Kellerman, who was really having fun. He was standing in his chair, waving a bottle of beer he'd inserted in his unzipped fly. He spotted me.

"Hey, Karshner, you sonofabitch. Wanna drink?"

He thrust the bottle toward me in an obscene gesture.

Everybody railed with laughter, beating the tables and the arms of their chairs. They roared, and thrashed and stomped. Smith even fell to the floor where he rolled around like a ball of uncontrollable jello, laughter tears streaming down his gin-lit face. Another wave of laughter surged through the group as Kellerman opened the bottle, and beer squirted from his imaginary bladder. Everyone howled, and why not? It was just one of the boys having a little fun.

More drinks were ordered, and more drinks, until everyone

had bought a round. Markham was getting redder by the second. His skin was the color of an unhealthy beet. I knew he had ulcers and all this liquor had to be devastating to his stomach, but he kept on drinking.

There always seems to be this compulsiveness at conventions. It's as though grown men are given a reprieve for a few days; as if they've been released from a cage, free to sweep the sky for a few golden hours before returning to the leash of responsibility. Sad, but there is this pressure, this compulsiveness to enjoy, to have fun. And have fun, they do to the detriment of their own welfare, their own dignity.

After what seemed days, the boys decided to move on to our hotel. And, after a brief scene over who would pick up the tab, we departed the lounge.

We hired one of the cigar-shaped limos—the kind with those little pull-down seats in the rear, to take us to Miami Beach. The whole party piled into the thing, Kellerman, Smith, James, the two girls, Blanchfield, Markham and I. We were jammed in tightly. The girls were sitting on Kellerman's and Smith's laps. We started our journey, which became an orgy on wheels.

We'd gone no more than a mile on the freeway when Kellerman began grabbing at the girls. He'd grab and they'd giggle and push him away. He'd make a lunge at one and the other would pinch him or tickle him. He was having a devil of a time and everyone was laughing and shouting at him. Smith, who was holding one of the girls, decided to even things up a bit, so he pinned her arms with a steely bear hug. This gave Kellerman the advantage he needed. He began to remove the girl's shoes and hose, throwing them wildly about the limo. Then he ripped off her underthings. Seized by the passion of the moment, he began to assault the girl with all the delicacy of a lusty mountain goat. The other girl was likewise subdued by James and Blanchfield, who fell upon her like gnawing leopards. What a sight—a 70-mile-an-hour orgy on a brightly lit Miami freeway. People tumbling around the back of the limo like clothes in a dryer. And the flesh rolled on, undulating over the causeway and into Miami Beach.

As we neared our hotel, the limo driver, a broad-minded sort, who had not taken his eyes off the road the whole trip, suggested that the boys pull themselves together. Discreetly, he pulled into an unlit, unattended parking lot. Bits of clothing were collected and donned. Ties straightened. Lipstick, brushes and combs flashed. In no time, the group restored itself to a condition of normal, sloppy drunkeness.

The boys and the hookers poured into the hotel like the bulls at Pamplona. Their clothing was askew and the girls looked hard and cheap under the garish lobby lights. Roars went up as other boys greeted the new arrivals with last name familiarity. Mystically, only last names are used by conventioneers, a strange and impersonalizing businessman's practice.

"Karshner. I'd like you to meet Jamison, our Minneapolis manager."

"Simpson, vice president of promotion, shake hands with Karshner, our Pittsburgh rep." or "Karshner, Pittsburg—Peterson, Altoona." Very military. Kids at Camp Crass.

Along one side of the lobby, long tables had been set up. On the tables were rows of white plastic name cards. The cards contained the names of the conventioning army, snappy identifications with cute salutations: "Hi, I'm Fred Zitz, Fresno."

The name tags were being pinned on new arrivals by two

girls in one-piece bathing suits. Blue and white satin "welcome" banners were stretched diagonally across their chests. The girls obviously were professional beauty queens, the type that make careers out of being "Miss Boat Show." They had beehive hairdos that were noticeably reinforced with several vats of hair spray, too much eye shadow, too much everything. Both were ideal candidates for bowling alley cocktail waitress positions, but to the boys they were gossamer goddesses, sweet symbols of sex that were madly in love with each and every one of them.

Many of the guys kissed the greeters. Several made "cute" gestures and passes. Kellerman gingerly goosed one of the girls, causing her to bloody her knee on the metal strip that lined the table top. And, naturally, everyone had "class" remarks:

"How'd you like to stick it in that, Herb?"

"Willya look at the pair on her?"

"Wonder if she knows I'm in love?"

After the pinning ceremony, the boys split off to pursue their pleasures. Some repaired to the bar. Some to card games and others hired cabs to continue their unrelenting quest for broads. A few retired, out of exhaustion or disgust. I retired out of both. I took the elevator to my floor, visions of showers and sheets tumbling through my head.

I left the elevator and headed for my room. About halfway down the corridor, I heard a powerful thundering sound that was apparently swelling in my direction. Suddenly, from around one of the hallway corners, a nude woman burst into view. She was running at full stride, clutching her clothes to her chest. Her breasts were alternately heaving over the garments. She sped past, oblivious to my presence, toward the exit door at the end of the hall. Almost, simultaneously, her pursuers exploded around the hall corner. Two guys, sprinting like athletes with arms pumping and genitals flopping. They tackled the girl before she could reach the stairwell. She put up a valiant struggle. She kicked and screamed and cursed and scratched. For a brief period I thought she would escape, but the fellows finally managed to immobilize her. They picked her up by the arms and legs and commenced their retreat back down the hall. As they passed me, one guy said, breathlessly, "A hundred bucks a night means *all* night."

What could I say? After all, the boys were just having fun.

Most of the boys "just have fun" at sales conventions. They loot and pillage and rape. They move into cities like bands of incensed savages; all hot and hairy from their long celibacy as average U.S. businessmen. Hotels aren't visited, they're occupied. Restaurants and clubs aren't patronized, they're captured. Girls aren't entertained, they're eaten alive. Personal property is smashed with Halloween vigor. Rooms are desecrated into ruinous heaps and card games are always in progress. Morning, noon and night key executives sit huddled in smoky bedrooms from which some players never leave for the duration of the convention. Drinking becomes a competitive marathon and booze is constantly in motion to fill seemingly bottomless pits. Orgies are opulent and tawdry and ever present. Girls of every description perform like obedient puppies acts of total depravation. The sexual hallucinogenics bend the mind.

The next morning, hangovers had settled like a pall over the coffee shop. Guys were in hideous states of alcoholic decay from their all-night festivals. Table talk recalled the excitement of conquests.

"Karshner, this here broad comes up to me in this here

bar, see? She's got tits out to here. Well, she sits down and crosses her legs and man, I'll tell you, I could see all the way to Cuba. So what the hell, I order a couple of drinks—next thing I know this broad's got her hand on my leg. Now, I know she's a hooker, but I can tell this time is different. She really had the hots for me."

At other tables the business boys were busy masticating sales-promotional problems and anecdotes along with their ham and eggs. These guys are equally as sick as the idiots that give themselves over to excesses of sex. Interestingly, their malady may be a more serious one, because it is their constant conversational companion. There's no relief for themselves or their acquaintances. Business is on their tongue always.

"I remember this little dealer down in Wheeling. Well, he had stock running out of his ass. He was a mark and all the salesmen hit him good. Well, one night I got in there late and the store was busy as hell. So, I hung around until closing time. Then we went down to a corner bar. Man, did he get loaded. I had pitched the guy all night and finally sold him a carload of phonographs. Put the sonofabitch out of business. I say, 'If they're going out, they'll go out with my products.' "

At another table there were some numbers boys. They're the guys who relate to product through reference to catalog numbers. These freaks pride themselves upon their catalog-memory prowess. And they test one another's powers of recollection.

"Okay, Jim, 392."

" 'Rainy Evening in Wilksborough' by Andre Felp."

"Right! How about 153?"

"Irving Smerk conducting the Hapsburg Harmonicas."

"Fantastic! How about BC-761?"

"Uhhh, oh, God, hmmm, gosh, I don't remember."

"Lampert McKenzie plays Oscar Bustvien—Vol. No. 2."

"Oh, shit! I should have remembered."

Tossing off catalog numbers casually in normal conversation is also very "in."

"I sold the sonofabitch three thousand pieces of TC-1846. I phoned in the order to the branch. Harry picked up the phone. I said, 'Harry, ship Ace Electronics three thousand pieces of TC-1846.' He said, 'What! Three thousand pieces of TC-1846! Johnson, you gotta be kidding?' "

After breakfast, we all filed into the meeting room. It was very austere and quite large. Long tables with chairs were lined in rows parallel to the speaker's platform. Each table was provided with pitchers of ice water and glasses. Scratch pads and pencils were spaced at every seat. On the speaker's dias there was a podium bearing the hotel's name, behind it a large projection screen and a flag. Suspended from the ceiling, directly over the screen, was a large, round sparkly placard which reflected "Welcome to Convention 19—."

The meeting was convened by our director of sales. He made some dry remarks about past, present and future, and some other "Old Glory" bromides about how wonderful it was to see such an august assemblage of devoted individuals. Then he introduced the president, who also spouted endless platitudes about dedication and spirit.

After the president left the podium, business solemnly began. Dull people presented their respective portions of the show with the articulation of lock-jaw victims. The special-products guy revealed all kinds of goodies about phonographs and discussed wattage and speaker sizes—and drunks yawned and ice pitchers tinkled. Our merchandising ace became maudlin over cardboard posters, and as he held his visual aids with tenderness, I thought I detected teary eyes. Giant ad mats were also displayed and special cover art was passed through the audience for its personal inspection—and the drunks yawned and poured ice water and passed the cover art.

During the lunch break, the boys resumed their boozing, broad-chasing and business discussions.

The afternoon session was no more enlightening than the morning's. It was sandy-dry. People who plan conventions must apply tremendous ingenuity to the creation of these tributes to boredom. All manner of gimmicks are utilized. But they fail because they are merely ornaments that re-package the same stale stories.

Our financial leader beefed up his show with spicy, slide insertions. Breasts would momentarily appear between per-centages and profits. Thighs would flash instantaneously during a sequence of quota figures. Buttocks would shine rosily between sales curves and flow charts. Smiling señoritas, lusty negresses, provocative mamselles, big-busted brünn-hildes took us on a travalog of mathematical sex. All that was lacking was the saccharin production music and the announcer's dulcet voice saying, "And now as the profits rise in the east and the collections sink in the west, we bid farewell to 98 percent of our returns for the fiscal year."

The boys loved the slides and when they made their brief appearances the guys hooted, hollered and whistled. A bunch of industry beaver shooters. A pitiful testimonial to our adult business world.

As the proceedings crawled on, there was less hooting and pitcher tinkling. The boys' heads, full of booze and images of broads, were beginning to nod. Restlessness and fatigue were setting in. But I knew when the meeting adjourned, the crowd would come to life like a sleeping monster and the boys would pour into the night, ready soldiers in a battle for self-degradation. I exhaled deeply and resigned myself to three more fun-filled days.

Other arms of the industry such as merchandising and broadcast factions have yearly conventions also. These are auspicious affairs that usually last anywhere from three to five days. Large, glamorous facilities are taken to house these conventions. And no expense is withheld to show the conventioneers a good time. Big budgets are allocated.

The last major blow-out I attended was held at one of the nation's most plush hotels—a truly lavish joint that had hot and cold running everything. I was attending as a delegate from my company. My job was to sit in on the meetings, attend seminars, lunches, dinners and, in general, be a smiling, cordial, charming (indeed), greeter.

All of the major record companies had similar representatives. In fact, the top, executive brass was in attendance to pay homage to their customers. So, the cream of our business was curdling all over the place. In lobbies, parlors, bars, restaurants, and those ever-loving hospitality suites, presidents, vice-presidents, merchandising and promotional personages were representational of their organizations. Nifty people in natty attire were charming manufacturer greeters. I was no exception. I, for once, was on my good behavior and I bowed and clicked with the aplomb of a Prussian cavalry officer.

For weeks before these happenings, the major record manufacturers plan their tactics with war-like grimness and purposeful determination. Every trick in the proverbial book is employed to insure a good showing at upcoming conventions. Idea mills grind out gimmicks that will entertain the conventioneers and make favorable impressions. Helicopters, bearing record companies' names and logos, are hired to whisk convention arrivals from airports to meeting sites. Fleets of courtesy rental automobiles are hired by manufacturers. Billboards, hyping new recorded products and heralding convention people, are rented and strategically placed for maximum impressions. Arrangements are made for little goodies; bottles of booze, theater tickets, tour passes, etc., and they're placed in the rooms as magnanimous gestures of "welcome."

The manufacturers apply heavy butter at these conventions in order to impress and win over the folks, because these are the people who are responsible for effective air play and mass merchandising. So, the record boys go all out. They buy and scrape and entertain the visiting firemen like wind-up monkeys.

I spent most of the first night at the convention greeting guests as they arrived for check-ins. It was a huge convention. People from all parts of the country spilled into the lobby like waves of disembarking infantrymen. All sizes and shapes. Mostly middle aged. The men were wrapped in vestments indigenous to such grand occasions. Official convention attire: a lot of shiny suits, hounds-tooth checked jackets, bright, flowered neckties, white loafers and electric blue slacks. One fellow typified the record biz merchandising man. He was a towering five feet in his raised alligator shoes. He was wearing a green iridescent suit with two-inch side vents (what these vents prove, I'll never fathom). His shirt was light green and his tie was a garish, green-on-green, wide nightmare. In his right hand was a giant cigar with a three-inch ash. It looked like a circumcised salami. The thumb of his left hand was hooked jauntily in the top of his trousers which girded his pear-shaped waistline. He was a regular merchandising praying mantis.

And then there were the wives. A gaggle of gossip-swapping, over-dressed biddies. All furry and funny looking. Teddy bears—penguins. Perfumed, waddling, little beavers. Each, it seemed, sported more jewelry than the other. Ear drops, pendants, necklaces and rings glimmered and glistened in an "out-shine your neighbor" contest. Yes, a contest. On one side of the lobby a pear-cut pendant was going against a clustered earring. The earring caught the first light and sent a left hook of radiance to the pendant's right facet. The pendant reeled momentarily, then rallied with a well-directed prismatic uppercut that tagged the cluster right on the ear button. And the battles raged across the lobby, careening off flashbulbs, windows and the bald heads of the merchandising moguls. Generally, the wives resembled those tiny, waddling toys—you know, the ones that teeter down inclined surfaces. They had skinny legs stuck in potato bodies and were covered with fur. Roly poly, blue-haired cupey dolls, all set for fun.

As I scanned the lobby, I could see the "working girls" had infiltrated the proceedings. Yes, the hookers were out in full force. All sizes, shapes and prices. The quarter tricks (twenty-five dollar hookers) were boldly obvious. They looked like their price tags—cheap. No underwear; painted. These girls were free-lance hookers who scab at all major conventions. They work independently without aid of pimps. They hang around the lobbies and bars and try to make "hits." I knew this convention would mean bad business for the quarter girls because a certain amount of decorum would prevail due to the presence of wives. "Wives" is a real dirty word to convention hookers. For they know wives enforce respectability. Unescorted guys are also more reluctant to "pay for play" when wives are present. They're afraid that the stories of their incontinencies will be spread or fed back to their own spouses by the conventioning female gossips and tattle-tales. So, convention hookers hate the wives because they know, if the wives weren't in attendance, the boys would lay a wet wash.

Hundred-dollar-and-up tricks, on the other hand, do well at these conventions. These girls, who work through "set-up pimps" are usually long, tall beauties with the healthy radiance of beach girls. They're young, intelligent and attractive, with the comely grace of the girl next door. More like Vassar students than hookers. These hundred-dollar tricks are usually the dates of the unescorted and single convention-going men, and accompany them to lunches, dinners and the other social functions. Many of the older guys squire these demure, freckle-faced whores throughout the conventions. Big daddys with their hundred-dollar daughters.

Key executives are always very cool about hooker connections, and every caution is exercised to avoid exposure. So the girls are "entertained" in the privacy of the executive suites. After all, how would clients react to the sight of a record biggee, running nude over a bevy of broads. Hardly a sales motivater.

Hookers are the core of convention entertainment and manufacturers, always willing to trade favors for potential air play and sales, supply the beef. Many times girls are flown to conventions at the manufacturers' expense. In these cases, the hookers are given a flat fee of say, two thousand dollars to entertain the disc jockeys or buyers. They're set up in a room in the convention hotel where they "take care of" a parade of excited, industry types. Sometimes, preconvention arrangements are made for hookers through central pimp contacts. These pimps are contacted by the manufacturer and arrangements are made regarding hooker types and prices. Example: Say a broadcasters' convention is going to be held in Atlanta. Well, the manufacturer will call the hooker wholesaler in that city. He'll give the pimp all the details regarding dates, hotels and meeting agendas. Types, prices and the number of hookers needed will also be negotiated. The pimp, in turn, handles all the details—just like inter-city auto renting, without the green stamps.

Some of the manufacturers' "hospitality girls" were evident in the hotel lobby that night. They were sidling up to their dates with beautifully faked captivation. And the hundred-dollar-and-up tricks were arm-in-arm with their sweet, old industry fools. And the quarter tricks were trolling the lobby and sitting sloppy-legged at the bars. And the new arrivals kept pouring in and the manufacturing boys greeted them with dollar-sign handshakes. Another convention was beginning.

16
The Sales Game

ROBINSON-PATMAN ACT

(a) That it shall be unlawful for any person engaged in commerce, in the course of such commerce, either directly or indirectly, to discriminate in price between different purchasers of commodities of like grade and quality, where either or any of the purchases involved in such discrimination are in commerce, where such commodities are sold for use, consumption, or resale within the United States or any Territory thereof or the District of Columbia or any insular possession or other place under the jurisdiction of the United States, and where the effect of such discrimination may be substantially to lessen competition or tend to create a monopoly in any line on commerce, or to injure, destroy, or prevent competition with any person who either grants or knowingly receives the benefit of such discrimination, or with customers of either of them: Provided, that nothing herein contained shall prevent differentials which make only due allowance for differences in the cost of manufacture, sale, or delivery resulting from the differing methods or quantities in which such commodities are to such purchasers sold or delivered: Provided, however, that the Federal Trade Commission, may, after due investigation and hearing to all interested parties, fix and establish quantity limits, and revise the same as it finds necessary, as to particular commodities or classes of commodities, where it finds that available purchasers in greater quantities are so few as to render differentials on account thereof unjustly discriminatory or promotive of monopoly in any line of commerce; and the foregoing shall then not be construed to permit differentials based on differences in quantities greater than those so fixed and established: And provided further, that nothing herein contained shall prevent persons engaged in selling goods, wares, or merchandise in commerce from selecting their own customers in bona fide transactions and not in restraint of trade: And provided further, that nothing herein contained shall prevent price changes from time to time where in response to changing conditions affecting the market for or the marketability of the goods concerned, such as but not limited to actual or imminent deterioration of perishable goods, obsolescence of seasonal goods, distress sales under court process, or sales in good faith in discontinuance of business in the goods concerned.

(b) Upon proof being made, at any hearing on a complaint under this section, that there has been discrimination in price or services or facilities furnished, the burden of rebutting the prima facie case thus made by showing justification shall be upon the person charged with a violation of this section, and unless justification shall be affirmatively shown, the Commission is authorized to issue an order terminating the discrimination: Provided, however, that nothing herein contained shall prevent a seller rebutting the prima facie case thus made by showing that his lower price or the furnishing of services or facilities to any purchaser or purchasers was made in good faith to meet an equally low price of a competitor, or the services or facilities furnished by a competitor.

(c) That it shall be unlawful for any person engaged in commerce, in the course of such commerce, to pay or grant, or to receive or accept, anything of value as a commission, brokerage, or other compensation, or any allowance or discount in lieu thereof, except for services rendered in connection with the sale or purchase of goods, wares, or merchandise, either to the other party to such transaction or to an agent, representative, or other intermediary therein where such intermediary is acting in fact for or in behalf, or is subject to the direct or indirect control, of any party to such transaction other than the person by whom such compensation is so granted or paid.

(d) That it shall be unlawful for any person engaged in commerce to pay or contract for the payment of anything of value to or for the benefit of a customer of such person in the course of such commerce as compensation or in consideration for any services or facilities furnished by or through such customer in

connection with the processing, handling, sale, or offering for sale of any products or commodities manufactured, sold, or offered for sale by such person,
unless such payment or consideration is available on
proportionally equal terms to all other customers com-
peting in the distribution of such products or
commodities.

(e) That it shall be unlawful for any person to
discriminate in favor of one purchaser against another
purchaser or purchasers of a commodity bought for
resale, with or without processing, by contracting to
furnish or furnishing, or by contributing to the furnishing of any services or facilities connected with the
processing, handling, sale, or offering for sale of such
commodity so purchased upon terms not accorded to
all purchasers on proportionally equal terms.

(f) That it shall be unlawful for any person engaged
in commerce, in the course of such commerce, knowingly to induce or receive a discrimination in price
which is prohibited by this section.

Essentially the Robinson-Patman statute is a safeguard
against discriminating price practices. It warns sellers not to
play with prices and demands equal pricing for buyers of
similar types.

As far as the record business is concerned though,
Robinson-Patman may as well be the names of boxing con-
testants or the names on a law firm door. The industry sales
guys avoid and circumvent the provisions as if they were the
gates on a down-hill slalom. Allow me to disclose some of the
practices employed by the industry sales sharks that under-

mine the foundations of good business and destroy the small, independent record retailers of America.

Naturally, the industry sales swingers must be exceedingly careful not to engage in overt price discrimination. They must be cautious, and so they give price breaks to the big users, about one hundred buyers, who represent, roughly, 80 percent of the industry's total billing, in carefully disguised ways. Here are some dandies.

Allowances for phony advertising is one method of giving extra illegal percentages. Let's take a hypothetical case.

A salesman calls upon an account. He offers the buyer an extra 10 percent on a 20,000 dollar purchase. He informs the buyer that the "extra ten" can be made up in the form of phony advertising, which his company will honor. Assuming the buyer accepts the deal, he will then bill the seller for $2,000-worth of illegitimate advertising by either (a) Taking in-store photographs of the manufacturers products and submitting the photos to the manufacturer, along with bills for "in-store merchandising display allowances" (these displays are merely set-ups and take-downs for photographic proof of merchandising), or (b) Submitting to the manufacturer a bill for $2,000 for handbill distribution (the buyer prints up three or four dummy handbills only, at a small cost, to submit as proof of advertising), or (c) Submitting to the manufacturer a bill for $2,000 for customer mailer inserts (again, only a token amount of dummy inserts are printed as proof of advertising tangibility).

And there are other means.

In some cases, accounts submit phony affidavits and tear sheets that are obtained from broadcasters and newspapers who will work with them. The accounts induce such favors by either committing all of their business to the stations and papers or by offering a kickback as payment for the mock-up affidavit and print ads. Many independent broadcasters and newspapers are particularly amenable to counterfeit billing ploys.

Sometimes, older tear sheets are submitted as proof of advertising participation. The dates are missing from these tear sheets, but if anyone questions their absence, the buyers just claim they were inadvertently ripped off when the tear sheets were pulled from the publications. But who questions?

Manufacturers also give extra discounts to big users through direct deductions. This is an extremely dangerous method however, and is usually avoided if at all possible. In some cases, though, when big billing on a consistent basis is available from a major account, the seller will acquiesce. The buyer is sworn to secrecy, though, because any invoice revelations would result in scorching FTC actions.

Free goods are sometimes given as extra percentage inducements. And unmarked promotional goods are withdrawn from stocks to make up extra "tens," "fifteens," and "twenties." Some buyers prefer free merchandise discounts due to the maximum profits that can be realized by retailing the goods. Extra percentages are computed at cost prices, so an extra 10 percent, for example, on a $25,000 order, would guarantee the buyer 1,000 units of his selection of a $2.50 per unit album item. Now, if the buyer retails the 2,500 units of free goods at $4.00 per selection, he will pick up $1.50 per album, which totals $3,750. This means, in effect, that the account actually received a 15 percent discount on a $25,000 purchase. Naturally, the accounts always select "cream" products as their free goods choices. (Big name and currently hot artists are always adversely affected by free-goods deals because they lose sales and, consequently, royalties.)

When possible, manufacturers prefer to make up shady

discounts with free goods due to low product costs. For example, an album only costs the manufacturer approximately 50¢ to produce. Therefore, it only costs $500 to offset a $2,500 extra percentage. Infinitely less costly than a direct or phony advertising credit issuance.

Larger accounts are also shown preference through pre-price increase offers. Say, for example, a manufacturer intends to raise his cost prices on January 1st. He will approach his major users on December 1st and inform them of the impending price hike. Of course, these buyers will "load in" at the lower prices and, therefore pick a tremendous discount advantage over uninformed customers. Shrewd buyers also load in the merchandise so they can return it for credit later at the new, increased cost prices.

Large users are also shown preferential treatment in regard to overages and deletes. "Overages" are excessive overstocks on particular selections, and "deletes" are selections that are removed from manufacturers catalogs due to slow sales movement. The manufacturers make exclusive offers to certain large accounts relative to overages which are dumped discreetly for 75¢ to $1.00 per album selection. These overage dumps represent good buys, even though they are not all "cream" items, due to the high mark-up and return potentials. Overages, keep in mind, are *not* cutouts. They are still active catalog selections and, therefore, acceptable exchange and return items. You can see the return advantage. A customer can make a clean $1.50 to $1.75 just for loading up and subsequently returning the merchandise. The manufacturers attempt to sell these overages on a no-return basis. These no-return stipulations are difficult to enforce, however, and the buyers, artfully, over a long duration, ease the merchandise back for full credit.

Deletes and cutouts are offered to all customers. The large

accounts still, however, get the first shot, and they usually, due to their capabilities to liquidate vast quantities of merchandise, buy up most of the goods. The smaller accounts really don't have a chance. Deletes aren't returnable, but they still represent a good profit buy for the big, multi-outlet merchandisers.

Artists, by the way, aren't paid royalties on cutouts, and availability of their merchandise at cheapy prices can jeopardize the sales of their current catalog items. Artists, as well as the small record retailers, are victimized by overage liquidations and cutout dumps.

Buyers for the major accounts are often offered personal cash and merchandise inducements. Merchandise incentives are usually explained away as contest prizes in order to divert any direct pay-off suspicion, and television sets, sporting-goods equipment, appliances and vacations are awarded for nonexistent contests.

There are also discriminatory advertising practices. Major account's advertising claims which are questionable are frequently approved by national sales departments.

Manufacturers invariably shade advantages to certain accounts and buyers. Disproportionate national advertising monies are given to larger accounts. And these larger accounts are also treated with carte blanche return privileges. One overt example of account preference was manifested when a major manufacturer hosted pet accounts at last year's Super Bowl game. All transportation, meals, lodging and ticket expenses were picked up for a privileged few.

Unrealistic credit privileges are also afforded some accounts, and some of the biggees are permitted to work on the company's dollars due to their abilities to buy and merchandise great quantities of product. Other smaller accounts however, are refused shipment due to small, overdue balances. A proportionate injustice.

Each year the industry's financial boys project better business. They always do, even when business and product are bad. But this is the dramatic, forward-looking, American way of doing business, and everybody must move forward into the 70s by expanding their goals and raising their sights. So the guys with the accounting degrees and the electric pencil sharpeners forecast bright futures out of grim realities, and figures are manipulated and books are rearranged and consumer lethargy, customer returns, bulging warehouses and stupid management are overlooked because—never forget it— the record industry is always dramatic, enthusiastic and excited.

These unrealistic projections that arise out of analyses made by unaware computer freaks, result in irrational fiscal sales projections, which result in impossible sales quotas that are achieved at great corporate losses. What? I'm sure you're thinking, how can you do more business and lose? Well, it's easy in an industry helmed by management teams that should be employed by Ringling Brothers, Barnum and Bailey to sweep up after the elephant act.

In order to achieve their unrealistic sales quotas, the record manufacturing sales heads and their field carbon snappers go to fantastic extremes to make their objectives. Extremes that are destroying the business.

Accounts, for example, are loaded with merchandise due to the manufacturers overreleasing and overselling. Each day more and more mediocre junk is jammed into the marketing pipelines where it backs up and sits dormant waiting to be returned. The wholesalers find it difficult to keep abreast of the flood and they stand knee deep in stuff that does little more than consume premium warehouse space.

But the releases keep coming and the deals keep flying and the hype rolls on.

In order to attain quotas, the manufacturers unload their new releases and catalog junk by offering deals and utilizing dishonesties that give stockholders hives.

Special deals and stocking programs are offered to customers as inducements to buy. Special advertising budgets are offered. Special discounts are volunteered and 100 percent return for credit privileges are granted (which means the buyers can return for credit all the crap they don't sell). In many instances, as I have disclosed earlier, anti-Robinson-Patman practices are instigated to get big business from big buyers.

Loading deals and guaranteeing are only some of the methods used to dredge up billing and hit quotas. Order padding is another means of hitting objectives and the field sales people pad orders to hit their targets and, therefore, relieve the constant national pressures for "quota or else" performances. So these industry Uriah Heeps pad customer orders and when the customers complain, the salesmen simply authorize the merchandise for full credit returns.

National sales offices also offer sales incentives to spark quota-busting performances from field sales guys. Special sales contests are also contrived to motivate salesmen and their customers. During these contests, every devious means is brought into play to win nice prizes like cars, cash, appliances, furs and sun-filled nights in Pago Pago. The salesmen and their accounts work together to win, and the salesmen offer fantastic terms to big buyers as stimulants for massive purchases. These contests are devastating to the corporate interest because they generate jaded prosperities and result in subsequent return monsoons. Big bonuses are paid and prizes awarded for the temporary billing.

End of the month quota-hitting fanaticism also results in false prosperity. Say a manufacturer's April sales quota is ten million dollars and on April 29 his sales records indicate that only eight million dollars worth of goods has been billed. Well, the national sales head will issue an ultimatum to his field management team (just like baseball) to "ship every goddamn thing in the warehouses." The field guys start shipping; anything, everything indiscriminately to their customers. Accounts that are primarily Country and Western outlets are shipped operatic music. Classical dealers are shipped bluegrass music and so on. Warehouse bins are cleaned and stocks are glutted in this mass picking, packing and shipping orgy that results in subsequent returns and credit issuances to the tune of—you guessed it—two million bucks. On the surface, though, all appears rosy. Quota has been achieved. Harrah for the corporate carpetbaggers.

Industry national sales magicians are always spouting sales figures that burgeon due to overloading techniques. They are always whipping out computer print-outs to impress their brass and to influence the trade publications. A tab run will show, for instance, that seventy-five thousand units of a particular item has been sold. What the bullshit numbers don't reveal, however, is that sixty thousand were forced up the wholesale rectum by special deals and the sixty thousand pieces are still suspended there awaiting a healthy return enema.

Repackaging is another industry trick to pick up needed billing and crack monstrous quotas. So, old, wilting evergreens are unearthed and repackaged and resold, remerchandised, readvertised and re-returned.

Christmas music is the sharpest example of industry holiday opportunism. Jesus, Mary and Joseph are shipped in mass quantities into the retail mangers of record merchandising. And if there's no room at the inn, you can bet your tinsel that space will be found in the stable for heaps of joyous holiday sounds. Yes, Christmas time is the time for all-out industry push. So the manufacturers load in guaranteed tons of recorded product. Yule time is the season to be unholy, and the American sales sleighs dash through the snow laden with deals and discounts. You can't believe the activity that is generated by the industry sales elves at Christmas time. They're an army of little pointy-eared wheelers and dealers, padding red and green order blanks that, come January, will just be—red.

Death is another way of sales life. The passing of major recording personalities are particularly beneficial industry windfalls. The industry must plant sales reps disguised as interns and orderlies in ailing artists' sick rooms and hospitals to discern conditions and to instantly relate passings. Because, it seems, even before next of kin can be notified, mass marketing plans are being mounted by sales, merchandising and promotional departments and a death campaign is sprung in order to take instant maximum advantage of customer sympathy and nostalgia. Old catalog stuff is resurrected. Deleted items are reactivated and new covers are ordered to repackage out-of-date numbers. Full page trade ads are purchased, radio spots produced and merchandising aids fabricated. And, of course, there is always—the memorial album.

And the pencil boys keep sharpening, the quota boys keep

busting and the product keeps rotating on the return-for-credit carrousel.

The warehouses of record America are exploding with obsolescence due to a sales over-kill activated by totally unrealistic industry projections. And the obsolescence continues to grow and strangle profits because industry sales management nurtures it in its dedication to attain impossible dreams. And markets are flooded and consumers are besieged with the oversold, overmerchandised, overadvertised dregs that are the residue of the big lie.

17
Machines

And so the Music Machine sputters along under its load of hype and bullshit, dishonesty, double dealing and track records. It sputters and shakes and grinds under the strain of insincerity and greed, and its wheels spin and its gears gnash against the weight of hypocracy.

And the crap keeps coming down the industry conveyor belt and the machine keeps grinding away and spewing out more records and albums more often.

And the broadcasters keep yelling and screaming and ringing bells and playing jingles and the record guys keep loading markets and falsifying sales. And the machine hammers on!

And the promoters keep lying and buying and crying and laying and paying while the sales snakes keep wiggling through the tall grass of oversaturated marketing to bite more ankles that are wading in junk-jammed warehouses. And the machine rasps on!

And the producers produce and rake off and run, and the royalties roll down hillsides of waste, and the records and albums keep coming, and the industry keeps releasing big piles of putrid plastic. And the kickback kicks the business in the balls, and when it doubles over, parasites pick its pockets. And the machine keeps on smoking!

And the hookers hook and the industry looks—a self-voyeur—and payoffs are paid and deals are made and the returns keep circling like shooting-gallery ducks. And the trades bend and the trends trend and the music publishers enter G-major clefs in their bank books. And the machine keeps puffing!

And the flesh peddlers keep selling artists by the pound and the industry puts its own thumb on the scales just to watch the numbers roll. And conventions are convened with golden gavels of disgust and awards are awarded to losers who win. And waste, as a way of life, is toasted by foggy-minded management malefactors. And still the machine drudges on!

And the music machine is just one little mechanism. There are many other similar machines—monstrous Machiavellian machines that are run by shifty, self-seeking incompetents, whose maladroit and devious practices nurture and per-petuate the growth of overpriced, inferior consumer goods and services.

And the machines grind on. Chug.

Chug.

Chug.

The End